DICTIONARY OF PSYCHOLOGY

About the Author

David Statt was born in Glasgow in 1942. His M.A. degree was in General, Experimental, and Social Psychology from Glasgow University, and his Ph.D was in Psychology/Social Psychology from the University of Michigan. He has concentrated on explaining the ideas of psychology and the related social and behavioural sciences to as wide an audience as possible. This book is his second effort in that direction; the first, also published by Harper and Row, was *Psychology: Making Sense*.

Dr. Statt's interest in the study of human behaviour has been enlivened by spells outside the academic world. While living in New York he worked for the United Nations and for the Social Science Research Council.

DICTIONARY OF PSYCHOLOGY

David Statt

BARNES & NOBLE BOOKS
A DIVISION OF HARPER & ROW, PUBLISHERS
New York, Cambridge, Philadelphia,
San Francisco, London, Mexico City,
São Paulo, Sydney

A Hardcover Edition of this work was originally published in
Great Britain by Harper & Row Limited under the title *A
Dictionary of Human Behaviour.*

DICTIONARY OF PSYCHOLOGY. Copyright © 1981
David Statt
Published simultaneously in Canada by Fitzhenry &
Whiteside Limited, Toronto.

First BARNES & NOBLE BOOKS edition published 1982

ISBN 0–06–463553–8

84 85 86 10 9 8 7 6 5 4 3 2

Phototypeset by Input Typesetting Ltd, London SW19 8DR
Printed and bound in Great Britain by The Pitman Press, Bath

PREFACE

This dictionary makes no claim to be comprehensive. Indeed it claims to be highly selective. Instead of trying to include 'everything' on human behaviour – an impossible task of questionable value to anyone – I have set out unashamedly to be as helpful as possible to people beginning the study of psychology and related disciplines by defining the terms they are most likely to want defined in the course of their reading. Many of the entries contain terms defined elsewhere in the book and these appear in SMALL CAPITALS for cross-reference.

In selecting entries I have been guided by terms currently in use in introductory textbooks and in popular writing in the field of human behaviour. The work being done in this field, and the terminology used to describe it, has changed at such a rapid rate that many terms in existing dictionaries are now obsolete.

I have also tried to bear in mind that my audience will be composed of intelligent people who have little or no training in the study of human behaviour. This may seem like a blinding glimpse of the obvious to you, but dictionaries of psychology seem traditionally to have been written with two different audiences in mind, illiterates and people with PhDs in experimental psychology. I have therefore assumed, for example, that you already know what faeces are and you don't particularly care to know what fascicles, fibrils, and fistulas are. This makes for a slim, but I hope useful, volume.

I'd like to express my thanks to Mike Forster of Harper and Row for suggesting such an enjoyable project to me, and to Kate Wenger for reading the manuscript intelligently while typing it with great despatch.

DAS

A

ablation   Surgical operation to remove part of the BRAIN.

abnormal   Can only be defined in relation to the term NORMAL, about which there is probably more disagreement than anything else in the field of human behaviour. In whatever sense it is used abnormal implies divergence from what is normal. It is generally used to describe someone's behaviour when it disturbs the regular course of his everyday life, or that of other people, especially if it results in his being put into a mental institution. People who believe they are Jesus Christ or who lie in a trance for days on end would be called abnormal by most mental health professionals.

   However, there is an important school of thought which believes that much, if not all, of the behaviour described as abnormal can be found in normal people from time to time, that mental institutions may be a convenient way for a society to get rid of people who are socially troublesome, that a society can itself in some sense be psychologically abnormal (the clearest example being Nazi Germany), and that 'going crazy' may be a way of escaping from intolerable social conditions. See FLIGHT INTO ILLNESS.

abnormal psychology   The field of PSYCHOLOGY that investigates and deals with BEHAVIOUR regarded as ABNORMAL. See also CLINICAL PSYCHOLOGY, PSYCHIATRY, PSYCHOANALYSIS and PSYCHOPATHOLOGY.

abreaction   The relief of tension that patients experience in PSYCHOANALYSIS when they relive a conflict or TRAUMA which they had REPRESSED. See also CATHARSIS.

1

absolute threshold   The point at which a stimulus can just be picked up by the sense organs.

absolutism, in moral development   According to PIAGET, a concern with rules about the world, as reflected in a child's play, begins around the age of five. At this stage, children have a blind faith in the rules and the ideas of right and wrong given them by their parents. Each child regards his or her parents as the ultimate arbiters of these rules which they perceive as being quite absolute, subject to no arguments, compromises, or changes of any kind.

accommodation   PIAGET's term for the way children alter their intellectual framework for dealing with the world when new experiences cannot be ASSIMILATED within it.

acculturation   The process by which people learn the assumptions, beliefs, and behaviour patterns of a CULTURE, either as children growing up in a certain time and place or as adults moving from one culture to another.

achieved status   A sociological term for describing a position that someone has achieved in society by his or her own efforts. Contrasted with ASCRIBED STATUS.

achievement, need for   See NEED FOR ACHIEVEMENT.

acquired characteristic   Originally used in GENETICS to describe a change that occurs in the physical structure of an organism as a result of its own activities or its interaction with the environment. Ie, a characteristic (like a bodybuilder's biceps) that is not INNATE. There has long been an argument as to whether acquired characteristics can be genetically transferred to offspring (see LAMARCKIANISM). Nowadays this argument is generally considered a loser, though interest in it may still revive. In PSYCHOLOGY, skills acquired by learning (like reading and writing) are sometimes referred to as acquired characteristics.

acquired drive   Sometimes used of MOTIVATION, the arousal or satisfaction of which has been learned.

acquired status   See ACHIEVED STATUS.

acrophobia   PHOBIA about heights.

acting out   A psychoanalytic term for the behaviour of a patient who has to act on a powerful and deep-rooted impulse, and is unable to reflect on it and talk about it instead.

actualizing tendency   Sometimes employed by HUMANISTIC PSYCHOLOGISTS in referring to the basic MOTIVATION of people to support and develop the self. See SELF-ACTUALIZATION.

acuity Literally, sharpness. Used in relation to the senses, eg, visual acuity.

adaptation Originally a biological term used to describe physical or behavioural changes that increased an organism's chances of survival. Used in PSYCHOLOGY to describe responses to changes in the environment. eg where the eye adjusts to changes in the light (see DARK ADAPTATION) or where the changed expectations of their society demand some kind of social adaptation in people's behaviour. See also ADJUSTMENT.

adaptation level The concept that an organism will perceive and interpret a particular stimulus within the context or frame of reference in which it was previously learned.

adaptation time The time taken for a sense organ to adapt to a stimulus, as measured by the time elapsed between the start of a steady stimulus and the cessation of any further response to it.

adaptive behaviour Behaviour intended to deal with changes in the environment. See ADAPTATION and ADJUSTMENT.

addiction Physiological and psychological DEPENDENCE on a drug in order to function. It implies both a physiological and psychological ADAPTATION to an altered normality.

adjustment Similar to ADAPTATION, especially in a social context, but usually implies a greater purposiveness and AWARENESS on the part of the individual faced with environmental demands.

Adler, Alfred (1870–1937) An early disciple of FREUD who founded his own movement in 1911, the first of Freud's major followers to break away. Adler disagreed with Freud's emphasis on the importance of sexuality to the human condition, preferring to stress the DRIVE for power and the need to compensate for deficiencies experienced by people in certain areas of their PERSONALITY – the source of the famous INFERIORITY COMPLEX.

adolescence Usually defined as the period of human development between the onset of puberty at around 12 years and the attainment of physical adult maturity at around 21 years; ie a biological definition. Emotional, moral, and intellectual development may not occur on the same time schedule. The interrelation of these different types of development gives this period its psychological importance. Adolescence is unique to our kind of society. Anthropologists and historians have found societies in which the onset of puberty is taken to mark the full transition from CHILDHOOD to adulthood, with no other period of preparation being thought necessary.

adrenalin Hormone secreted by the adrenal glands, (which are situated on top of the kidneys), in times of emergency or excitement. It increases the heart rate, the blood supply, the sugar supply from the liver into the blood stream and alerts the muscles to impulses from the nervous system, thereby getting the organism ready for 'FIGHT OR FLIGHT'. Alternative name is EPINEPHRINE.

aesthesiometer An instrument for quantifying skin sensitivity to touch by measuring the smallest distance between two points of contact on the skin where the person can perceive each of them separately rather than as a single stimulus.

aetiology The study of the origins of disease: physical, mental, or emotional.

affect Widely used in PSYCHOLOGY for feeling and EMOTION.

afferent The process of carrying information from the sense organs through the nerves to the BRAIN. Contrasted with EFFERENT.

affiliation, need for See NEED FOR AFFILIATION.

after-image A visual impression that persists after the stimulus has been removed, eg when the eyes are closed after looking at a bright light.

age-grading The process of dividing the members of a society into groups according to their ages, applying labels to these groups (infants, teenagers, senior citizens, etc), and expecting the members of each group to behave in certain characteristic ways. This process is perhaps most clearly seen when people do not behave in the manner expected of them. For example, a child in solemn mood may be described as a 'little old man', or a middle-aged person whooping it up may be having a 'second childhood'. Age-grading is found in all societies, though the gradations and the expectations of behaviour that accompany them vary enormously.

ageism Like racism and sexism, ageism is discrimination against people because of an attribute arbitrarily determined by birth – age.

agnosia A failure of PERCEPTION caused by BRAIN DAMAGE. The sufferer is unable to recognize familiar objects or make sense out of sensory information.

agoraphobia PHOBIA about open spaces.

aha reaction   A sudden insight, the kind that often accompanies the exclamation 'aha!' (in German, too, apparently for the phrase was introduced by Wolfgang KOHLER). It is used to describe the moment when the solution to a problem appears or the disparate elements of a situation suddenly add up to a meaningful pattern. See also GESTALT and GESTALT PSYCHOLOGY.

Figure 1   Aha reaction. Using the shorter sticks, the chimpanzee pulls in a stick long enough to reach the piece of fruit. He has learned to solve this problem by understanding the relationship between the sticks and the piece of fruit.
(from *Introduction to Psychology*, 4th edition, E R Hilgard and R C Atkinson, New York, Harcourt, Brace Jovanovich, 1967, p 302)

alexia   Word blindness. The loss of the ability to read, through BRAIN DAMAGE.

alienation   A term with various shades of psychological and sociological meaning all of which refer in common to feelings of being estranged, separated, and powerless, whether in relation to oneself, to nature, to other people, to wealth and the means of production in a society, or else to society as a whole. See also EFFICACY.

all-or-none principle   Used in PHYSIOLOGICAL PSYCHOLOGY to

5

describe the way a nerve responds to stimulation. Either the stimulus is inadequate and the nerve does not respond at all, or it responds to its maximum capacity.

alpha rhythm   The type of BRAIN WAVES found in adults when they are resting. They have an average FREQUENCY of ten per second.

altercasting   Term used by some social psychologists to describe the process of trying to get someone to play the ROLE you want them to.

alter ego   A literary term, meaning 'the other I', for a person who seems to exemplify another version of oneself.

altered states of consciousness   Situations in which one's SUB-JECTIVE experience is different from normal waking CONSCIOUS-NESS. These alterations can be caused by drugs or stimulants or emotional upheaval or a combination of these. Religious ecstasy is a common type of altered state, and is often accompanied by visions and other mystical experiences.

altruism   The opposite of selfishness; being concerned for others rather than oneself (or one's SELF).

ambiguity, tolerance for   See TOLERANCE FOR AMBIGUITY.

ambiguous figures   A drawing that appears to change as you look at it and become something else. The two figures alternate automatically as the perceptual system recognizes first one then the other. It is not possible to perceive both at the same time.

Figure 2 Ambiguous figures

ambivalence   Tendency to oscillate between opposing types of behaviour, opinions and, especially, feelings about someone.

amnesia   Loss of MEMORY, either through BRAIN DAMAGE caused by accident, alcohol or drugs, or through emotional STRESS. Amnesia may be total or partial, but unless it results from severe brain damage, the lost memories are usually recoverable. See also DISSOCIATION and REPRESSION.

amnesia, infantile   See INFANTILE AMNESIA.

anaesthesia   Loss of sensitivity to stimulation which may be total (as when a general anaesthetic is given before surgery) or local. A local anaesthetic may also be given for minor surgery. Local anaesthesia which is not artificially induced in this way is psychological in origin. It may be known as glove or shoe or stocking anaesthesia to indicate the part of the body affected. This kind of anaesthesia is a symptom of HYSTERIA.

anal stage   According to SIGMUND FREUD this is the second STAGE in an infant's life, when he is mainly concerned with the pleasure he receives from the anus and its function. Anxiety caused by toilet training may overlay the infant's pleasure. As with all of Freud's stages, excessive frustration or satisfaction at the anal stage may leave a person fixated on it, with the eventual result that, as an adult, he may exhibit an 'anal' character, typified by obstinacy, tidiness and miserliness.

analogies test   A widely used type of mental test which asks the subject to complete the fourth term, eg, 'champagne is to France as caviar is to. . . .'

analysand   Someone undergoing PSYCHOANALYSIS.

analysis   See PSYCHOANALYSIS.

analysis of variance   Statistical technique for determining whether the differences found in a DEPENDENT VARIABLE in an EXPERIMENT are greater than can be expected by chance.

analyst   See PSYCHOANALYST.

androgynous   Tendency of a male body to show female physical characteristics. Sometimes used the other way around.

angst   German word meaning ANXIETY. It was introduced by early PSYCHOANALYSTS and is sometimes found in modern literature.

animism   The belief that inanimate natural objects (like rocks or rivers) are animate living things, or contain souls or spiritual forces.

anomie Term introduced by the French sociologist Emile Durkheim to describe a condition of society where SOCIAL NORMS are breaking down and people may become confused both about their place in that society and about their sense of IDENTITY in general.

anorexia A lack of appetite which is really a COMPULSION to avoid eating food. It is most often found in teenage girls and in extreme cases can result in death by starvation.

anthropocentric Acting on the unquestioned assumption that man is the centre of the universe.

anthropology The study of the different physical and cultural conditions of mankind.

anthropomorphism The tendency to see human qualities in gods or animals.

antisocial personality Characterized by lack of conscience. Such a person has not internalized the values of his society and seems to feel no GUILT or ANXIETY in behaving criminally, and even committing murder. Often accompanied by a tendency to gratify needs impulsively that results in chronic conflict with society. Also referred to as 'psychopath' or 'psychopathic personality'.

anxiety A term used with many shades of meaning and in many different areas of PSYCHOLOGY. It is generally held to be an unpleasant emotional state resulting from STRESS or conflict and characterized by fear and apprehension. If the fear and apprehension are vague and diffuse and not attached to a specific object, or if they seem excessive, the anxiety is considered NEUROTIC.

aphasia Loss of ability to use language (especially the ability to speak) because of BRAIN DAMAGE.

Apollonian Anthropological concept borrowed from ancient Greece where the sun god Apollo represented the reasonable, rational, and intellectual aspects of the human condition. Contrasted with DIONYSIAN.

apparent movement A visual ILLUSION in which the BRAIN perceives movement when there is none. See PHI PHENOMENON.

apperception The final stage in the process of PERCEPTION where something is in the forefront of one's ATTENTION and is clearly recognised or understood.

approach-approach conflict Caused by having to choose between two desirable objects or goals.

approach-avoidance conflict Caused by being confronted with an object or goal that is at the same time both attractive and unattractive (like delicious Chinese food that gives you heartburn).

aptitude The potential for acquiring a skill or ability after some training.

aptitude test An instrument that tries to predict a person's capacity for acquiring a certain skill or ability.

arc of human possibilities Anthropological term for the whole range of human potential. Different societies develop different aspects of the human condition, and will therefore fall at different places on the arc. While there will always be some overlap between any two societies, no two societies will ever overlap completely.

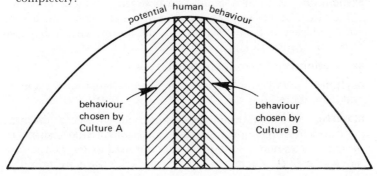

Figure 3 An arc of human potential

archetype JUNG's term for the contents of what he called the COLLECTIVE UNCONSCIOUS, a set of behaviour patterns that were supposedly passed on from generation to generation as the common heritage of mankind. Evidence for this archetype, according to Jung, lay in the similarity of symbols in different CULTURES across time and place for fertility, birth, death, and so on.

Army Alpha Test The first INTELLIGENCE TEST to be used en masse – by the United States army during World War One; designed for literate English speakers.

arousal level Physiological term that describes how alert the BRAIN of a person or animal is to messages about the external world coming to it via the senses.

asceticism A way of life in which people deny themselves sen-

9

sual pleasures in order to concentrate on what they consider a more important intellectual or spiritual life.

ascribed status   A sociological term for describing a position in society given to someone automatically because of something he or she has inherited at birth (like skin colour or family background). Contrasted with ACHIEVED STATUS.

assertiveness training   A technique of BEHAVIOUR MODIFICATION intended to help people overcome INHIBITIONS about expressing their feelings. Involves a lot of ROLE PLAYING.

assimilation   PIAGET's term for the way children absorb experiences from their environment and give them meaning within their existing intellectual framework. Contrast with ACCOMMODATION.

association   A learned connection between two ideas or events. One of PSYCHOLOGY's oldest and most general concepts, it goes back at least as far as Aristotle in the fourth century BC. See LAWS OF ASSOCIATION.

association test   See WORD ASSOCIATION TEST.

asylum   Literally, a place of refuge. An obsolete term for a mental institution.

atavistic   Genetic term for the reappearance of a TRAIT that was not present in the most immediate ancestors of an organism. In PSYCHOLOGY and the SOCIAL SCIENCES it is used to describe BEHAVIOUR that is considered to be a throwback to a more primitive way of functioning.

attachment   An emotional bond with another person that is usually powerful and long-lasting. Used especially about the relationship between infant and mother. See DEPRIVATION and SEPARATION ANXIETY.

attention   The process of selecting one aspect of the complex sensory information from the environment to focus on, while disregarding others for the time being.

attitude   A stable, long-lasting, learned predisposition to respond to certain things in a certain way. The concept has a *cognitive* (belief) aspect, an *affective* (feeling) aspect, and a *conative* (action) aspect. See COGNITION, AFFECT and CONATION.

attitude scale   A set of questions designed to elicit ATTITUDES and measure their strength.

attribution   The process of trying to interpret and understand the human condition (our own and other people's) on the basis of overt BEHAVIOUR. We do this by attributing certain intentions or MOTIVATIONS to the people whose behaviour we observe. This is a social psychological concept that is really a way of describing what PSYCHOLOGY is all about. In a sense, it is the layman's equivalent of what the psychologist does.

authoritarian personality A person characterized by a concern with obedience and various TRAITS that seem to be associated with it, such as low TOLERANCE FOR AMBIGUITY, high PREJUDICE, rigid adherence to conventions, superstition, servility, and contempt for weakness.

autistic Description of a child possibly suffering from a form of SCHIZOPHRENIA, who is characterized by being withdrawn and unable to form relationships with people, to respond to environmental stimuli, or to use language. Adult thinking is sometimes described as autistic if it is guided by FANTASY, and WISH-FULFILMENT rather than OBJECTIVE reality.

autokinetic effect The ILLUSION that a small spot of light seen in a totally dark room is slowly moving about. It disappears when the light is seen in relation to the room.

autonomic conditioning CONDITIONING involuntary functions controlled by the AUTONOMIC NERVOUS SYSTEM, such as digestion, heart rate, or salivation.

autonomic nervous system The part of the nervous system that deals with the regular functioning of the human organs that are not usually under voluntary control, including the heart, lungs, digestion, etc. Compare with CENTRAL NERVOUS SYSTEM.

autonomy stage The second of the eight stages of development through the human life cycle proposed by ERIK ERIKSON. This stage occurs between the ages of one or one and a half years and three or three and a half years. It is the time concerned with acquiring self-mastery and overcoming feelings of doubt and shame. See EPIGENESIS and STAGE THEORIES.

autosuggestion A suggestion coming from oneself with the object of attempting, consciously, to produce a change in one's BEHAVIOUR.

aversion therapy A BEHAVIOURIST technique that attempts to eliminate some undesirable behaviour by the use of unpleasant stimuli, often electric shocks, for example by presenting an alcoholic with a bottle and a shock, until the bottle ceases to be a desirable object. See also CONDITIONING.

avoidance Tendency to withdraw from psychological conflict, often by substituting other, non-threatening activities.

avoidance-avoidance conflict Caused by having to choose between two undesirable objects or goals.

awareness Knowing that you are experiencing something. Apart from strict BEHAVIOURISTS most psychologists would call this CONSCIOUSNESS.

B

babble Speech sounds made by infants from which recognizable language develops.

Babinski reflex A normal reflex that occurs in infants below the age of two and then disappears. The toes curl upwards when the sole of the foot is stroked. If the Babinski reflex reappears in adulthood, it is a sign of a disorder in the nervous system.

balance theory According to the American psychologist Fritz Heider people have a tendency towards compatibility in their beliefs because incompatibility causes tension. For example, if you believe someone is gentle and you see him acting violently, your beliefs are in a state of imbalance. You would strive to balance them again, and this might be done by saying that the act was not really violent, or the person was not as gentle as you thought, or he was not responsible for his behaviour. See COGNITIVE DISSONANCE.

bandwagon effect SOCIAL PSYCHOLOGICAL term for the behaviour of people who feel a need to conform to the ATTITUDES or actions of a group they identify with. In the general parlance of SOCIAL SCIENCE the term is used to describe increasing support for a popular movement, where more and more people want to 'join the bandwagon'.

Bard-Cannon theory A neurological theory of EMOTION which proposes that stimuli from the environment trigger off responses in the HYPOTHALAMUS which alert both the BRAIN and the AUTONOMIC NERVOUS SYSTEM. The key point of this theory, in contrast to the JAMES-LANGE theory, is that the feelings associated with emotion come from the hypothalamus and these feelings are experienced first before we recognize them cognitively. So, for example, we cry *because* we are sad.

basic mistrust According to ERIK ERIKSON the pain of being thrust out of the all-supporting womb and into the harsh external world produces a state of basic mistrust in ourselves and in the world. Our first developmental task is therefore to acquire a sense of BASIC TRUST.

basic personality A concept proposed by the American social anthropologist Abraham Kardiner that the patterns of PERSONALITY characteristics will be similar for most people of a given society because of their similar CHILDHOOD experiences, and they would therefore share unconsciously-held unquestioned assumptions about life.

basic trust According to ERIK ERIKSON the acquisition of a sense of basic trust in oneself and in the world is the major task to be accomplished during the first 12 to 18 months of life. Basic trust is acquired if the infant's physical needs are met, if NORMAL biological maturation occurs, and most important, if the infant is loved and cared for by a mother who is herself trusting and self-confident. See also STAGE THEORY.

battle fatigue A state of psychological disorder resulting from the exhaustion, STRESS and ANXIETY of warfare. It can usually be cured after the patient is removed from the scene of the battle.

becoming A key concept of EXISTENTIAL PSYCHOLOGY. It describes the process of individual development leading towards the goal of being as human as possible, fulfilling as much of one's potential as possible, and being at one with the world. See also LAING.

Bedlam Probably a corruption of St Mary of Bethlehem, a hospital for mental patients founded in London in the 16th century. Because of this association the name has been popularly used for any place in a noisy, chaotic state, or any condition of wild disorder.

behaviour Any act of an animal or human. See BEHAVIOURISM and PSYCHOLOGY.

behavioural science The study of the behaviour of humans and animals by EXPERIMENT and observation. Centred around PSYCHOLOGY but branching out into biology and physiology on the one hand, ANTHROPOLOGY and SOCIOLOGY on the other (figure 4).

Behaviourism A school of PSYCHOLOGY founded in the United States by J B WATSON in 1913 as a reaction against a prevailing

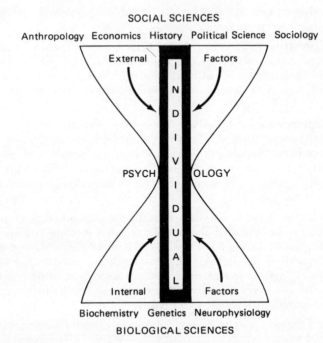

Figure 4 Behavioural science

(European) emphasis in academic psychology on the CONSCIOUS examination of the contents of the MIND (see WUNDT). Watson believed that the work of PAVLOV on CONDITIONING represented the future of psychology which should give up all talk of MIND and CONSCIOUSNESS and deal solely with the OBJECTIVE study and manipulation of human and animal behaviour. Watson is now generally regarded by psychologists as much too extreme and simple-minded, having been superseded by B F SKINNER and other more subtle theorists. Nonetheless the crucial emphasis on observable behaviour remains and flourishes. In a sense, every psychologist who performs an EXPERIMENT is a behaviourist in fact, if not in theory. For cultural and historical reasons behaviourism has continued to flourish more in the United States than elsewhere.

behaviour modification   The deliberate changing of a particular pattern of behaviour by behaviourist methods. See AVERSION THERAPY and OPERANT CONDITIONING.

behaviour therapy   A form of PSYCHOTHERAPY based on the assumptions of BEHAVIOURISM and using behaviourist means to eliminate undesirable behaviour. Its objective is therefore to remove the overt symptoms of the patient's difficulties. See also AVERSION THERAPY. Compare with CLIENT-CENTRED THERAPY and PSYCHOANALYSIS.

belief system A set of mutually supportive beliefs held by an individual or group.

bell-shaped curve Describes the shape of the curve obtained by plotting the FREQUENCY of a NORMAL DISTRIBUTION.

Bender-Gestalt Test A test for BRAIN DAMAGE which requires the subject to copy some simple designs.

berdache An American Indian term for a man who prefers the dress and style of life of a woman. Sometimes used by CLINICAL PSYCHOLOGISTS for a TRANSVESTITE.

Bernreuter Personality Inventory One of the earliest PAPER-AND-PENCIL TESTS of PERSONALITY (dating from the 1930s), which attempted to tease out the different aspects of the term.

beta rhythm BRAIN WAVES associated with mental activity rather than with resting. They appear as shallower and more frequent than those of the ALPHA RHYTHM.

biased sample Term used in social surveys or any area where a conclusion is to be made about a large POPULATION. The sample of the population being studied is considered biased if it is unrepresentative of the population as a whole, eg, if you say something about national opinion on a certain topic after interviewing your friends.

bilateral transfer Transferring a skill learned on one side of the body to the other side. For example, right footed people learning to kick with their left feet. See LATERALITY.

bimodal distribution A FREQUENCY DISTRIBUTION that has two MODES.

Binet, Alfred (1857–1911) A French psychologist who was asked by the Paris school system to find some way of predicting which children would not do well in school (and thus by implication those who would). To accomplish this task he invented and standardized the first example of what came to be called an INTELLIGENCE TEST. See also BINET SCALE and STANFORD-BINET.

Binet scale A series of items invented by BINET for predicting a child's performance in school. The items were arranged in order of difficulty and standardized by age. See also STANFORD-BINET.

binocular disparity Each of our eyes (because they are a few inches apart) receives a slightly different picture when looking at the same object. This disparity helps us perceive the dimension of depth. See DEPTH PERCEPTION and VISUAL CLIFF.

binocular fusion The way the BRAIN fuses the different images from each of our eyes into one visual PERCEPTION, so that we are quite unaware of the BINOCULAR DISPARITY.

biofeedback A technique for teaching someone to be aware of his physiological and BRAIN processes by giving him information about them as they occur. The aim of giving him this feedback is to help him control a particular process, like blood pressure, BRAIN WAVES, or heart rate. Often used to help someone relax by showing him a visual display of his brain waves and encouraging him to maintain the ALPHA RHYTHM.

biosocial The interaction of biological and social factors in the study of society, eg the social effects of birth rate or bubonic plague.

birth order The order of birth of the children in a family. Psychologists have long been interested in the possible connections between birth order and PERSONALITY TRAITS but so far the evidence is slight. See NEED FOR AFFILIATION.

birth trauma The shock of the sudden transition from the security and comfort of the womb to the harsh insecurity of the outside world. Some PSYCHOANALYSTS believe this to be the source of adult ANXIETY and something that must be dealt with before a person can become psychologically mature and free of NEUROSIS.

bisexuality Possessing the physical or psychological characteristics of both sexes. Also used now to mean sexual responsiveness to both men and women.

black box Used in scientific theorizing to indicate something that seems to work though nobody knows how it works or what goes on inside the 'box'. It is often used as an analogy for the BRAIN, or in a more general sense for any EXPERIMENT in PSYCHOLOGY where the input is controlled, the output is observed, and an inference made from the one to the other to account for what has happened in between.

Blacky pictures A PROJECTIVE TECHNIQUE, for disturbed children, using cartoons about a family of dogs (with a central character called Blacky). The cartoons portray relationships found in human families. The child is asked to make up stories about the cartoons and these are scanned for evidence of emotional problems.

Bleuler, Eugen (1857–1939)   Swiss PSYCHIATRIST and early follower of FREUD. Invented the term SCHIZOPHRENIA.

blind spot   The area of the RETINA where the OPTIC NERVE leaves the eye. This area is insensitive to light and the eye is therefore 'blind' at that point. Also used now to refer to an area of someone's (otherwise rational) beliefs which is impervious to change through OBJECTIVE information or rational argument.

body image   The picture a person has of how his body appears to other people. This image develops early in life and because of bodily changes it may, in later life, be markedly inaccurate. Body image is at the root of one's SELF-IMAGE.

body language   NON-VERBAL COMMUNICATION with other people by means of physical postures, movements, or GESTURES, that may be CONSCIOUS or UNCONSCIOUS.

Bogardus scale   The first written SOCIAL DISTANCE SCALE, invented by the American psychologist Emory Bogardus.

bonding   The process whereby people are linked together in a socially cohesive group, used especially of the emotional bonding between mother and infant. See BOWLBY.

boomerang effect   A term used by social psychologists in the study of attitude change. It refers to someone who changes his ATTITUDE in the opposite direction from that being advocated to him,

borderline   When used of mental ability it is usually defined as an IQ score between 70 and 80. In CLINICAL PSYCHOLOGY it is sometimes used to describe someone whose emotional disturbance appears to be more severe than NEUROSIS but is not quite PSYCHOSIS.

Bowlby, John (born 1907)   British PSYCHIATRIST who pioneered the study of the effects of MATERNAL DEPRIVATION on young infants.

brain   The part of the CENTRAL NERVOUS SYSTEM contained within the skull. It is the most complex and least understood part of the human body. Because of the brain's organizing role in all human behaviour it is sometimes compared to a central computer which stores, retrieves, and utilizes information. But the brain is infinitely more complex and powerful than that. In a sense our brain is what makes us human. All the limitless forms of human behaviour are a direct result of the brain's capacity (figure 5).

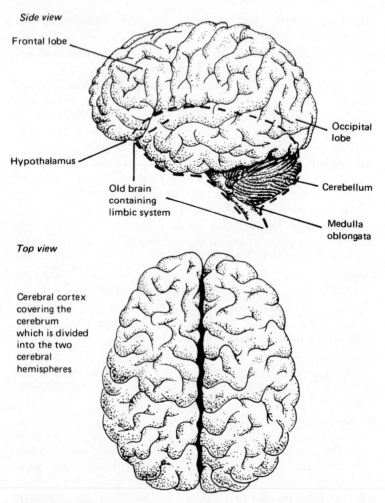

Side view

Frontal lobe

Occipital lobe

Hypothalamus

Old brain containing limbic system

Cerebellum

Medulla oblongata

Top view

Cerebral cortex covering the cerebrum which is divided into the two cerebral hemispheres

Figure 5 The brain

brain damage Any physical injury to the BRAIN, whether by accident, disease, drugs, or surgery; usually results in impairment of behaviour and emotional disturbance.

brain localization The controversial HYPOTHESIS that specific mental experiences or functions are associated with specific areas of the BRAIN.

brain potential In BRAIN physiology, the level of electrical activity in the brain.

brain stimulation The electrical stimulation of certain parts of the BRAIN in order to study their functions.

brainstorming In SOCIAL PSYCHOLOGY it refers to the free generation of ideas by the members of a group for the purpose of solving a specific problem.

brainwashing An attempt to coerce someone into radically changing his beliefs or behaviour by using physical, psychological, or social pressures.

brain waves The recorded rhythms of the electrical activity of the BRAIN.

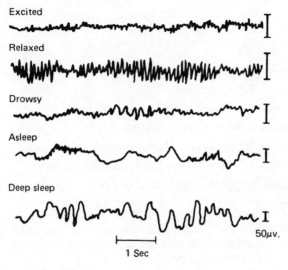

Figure 6 Brain waves
(from H. H. Jasper *Encephalography* in W. Penfield and T. C. Erikson *Epilepsy and Cerebral Localisation*, Charles C. Thomas, Springfield, 1941)

breakthrough Used in PSYCHOTHERAPY to describe a patient's sudden insight about a problem after he overcomes his RESIST-ANCE to dealing with it. See also ABREACTION and AHA REACTION.

brightness constancy The experience of PERCEIVING an object as maintaining the same level of brightness even though the OBJECTIVE illumination seen by the eye may change.

Broca's area The part of the BRAIN most closely involved with speech. Sometimes referred to as the SPEECH CENTRE. It is situated in the left hemisphere of all right handed people (ie over 90% of the population), though not in many left handed people.

Buhler tests Tests of infant development.

bystander apathy Refers to the tendency of people in a social situation not to go to the aid of strangers in an emergency. Apparently the more bystanders there are the greater may be the apathy because responsibility is then perceived as more diffuse and not vested in any one individual.

C

CA Chronological age. Used along with MENTAL AGE in computing an IQ score.

CAI See COMPUTER ASSISTED INSTRUCTION.

California F Scale See F SCALE.

California Infant Scale Tests of infant development.

Cannon-Bard theory See BARD-CANNON THEORY.

castration complex According to FREUD, a COMPLEX caused in men by UNCONSCIOUS fears of losing their penis, and in women by the fantasy of once having had a penis and then losing it. This complex supposedly has a universal origin in CHILDHOOD ANXIETY about being castrated as a punishment for harbouring sexual desires. See also PENIS ENVY.

CAT See CHILDREN'S APPERCEPTION TEST.

catalepsy A state of muscular rigidity, associated with severe psychological disturbance, or a hypnotic trance, where a person whose body or limbs are placed in a certain position will maintain that position for a long period of time.

cataplexy Immobility caused by fear or shock. Not to be confused with CATALEPSY.

catatonic Descriptive of PSYCHOTIC state generally considered to be a form of SCHIZOPHRENIA. Characterized by violent changes in BEHAVIOUR from mainly rigid, frozen states (including CATALEPSY) to occasional extremes of excitement and activity.

catharsis Ancient Greek term for the purging of EMOTIONS by seeing them enacted on the stage. In PSYCHOTHERAPY (particularly PSYCHOANALYSIS) it is used generally to describe the release of emotional tension when a conflict is overcome or an insight achieved (see ABREACTION). It is used in literature to describe emotional relief in general.

cathexis   Used mainly in PSYCHOANALYSIS to refer to the psychic energy a patient invests in a person, place, idea or thing. EMOTIONS associated with the object of cathexis may be keenly aroused whenever it is re-encountered.

censorship   In PSYCHOANALYSIS, the regulation of the REPRESSED material in the UNCONSCIOUS to see that nothing threatening to the EGO is allowed to escape into CONSCIOUSNESS. Censorship is apparently relaxed during sleep when repressed material is expressed in the form of DREAMS.

central nervous system   The part of the nervous system protected by bone, ie, the BRAIN and the spinal chord. It regulates all behaviour, thought, and internal bodily processes.

central organizing trait   According to the American psychologist Gordon Allport, a TRAIT that is characteristic of an individual's PERSONALITY and associated with many other traits. For example, the descriptions 'warm' or 'cold' are thought to be key terms.

central tendency   See MEASURE OF CENTRAL TENDENCY.

centering   In GESTALT PSYCHOLOGY, the perfect INTEGRATION of an organism and its environment.

cephalocaudal   Literally, head-tail. Usually refers to the process of maturation in humans and animals where the sequence of physical development proceeds from the head downwards. See PROXIMODISTAL.

cerebellum   Part of the BRAIN, at the back near the top of the spinal cord. It is thought to be involved in maintaining muscle tone and coordinating movement and balance.

cerebral cortex   The surface layers of grey matter that cover most of the BRAIN. Thought to be the area of the brain primarily concerned with the higher mental processes like learning, memory, and thinking.

cerebral dominance   The tendency for one CEREBRAL HEMISPHERE or the other to be dominant in its regulation of BEHAVIOUR − the left hemisphere in right handed people, the right in left handed people.

cerebral hemispheres   The two symmetrical left and right halves of the CEREBRUM. The right hemisphere controls the left side of the body, the left hemisphere the right side. See SPLIT-BRAIN TECHNIQUE.

cerebrum The main division of the BRAIN in all vertebrates but much more highly developed in humans than in any other. It is thought to be crucially involved in processing sensory information and in all forms of cognitive activity. See COGNITION.

cff See CRITICAL FLICKER FREQUENCY.

change agent A term that is sometimes used by people who try to apply SOCIAL PSYCHOLOGY to social situations. It refers to someone whose task is to stimulate social change in what is considered a desirable direction. For example, raising the CONSCIOUSNESS of an exploited group to the point of understanding and attempting to remove the exploitation.

character armour A concept, suggested by the PSYCHOANALYST Wilhelm Reich, that to protect his EGO an individual can put up a powerful front which dominates his whole PERSONALITY. For example, disguising hatred as love in dealing with a spouse or parent. Reich regarded the piercing of this armour as a key task for PSYCHOANALYSIS. See also REACTION FORMATION.

character disorder A BEHAVIOUR disorder characterized by immaturity and a general inability to cope with adult life. It often takes the form of social problems like alcoholism, drug addiction, or criminal behaviour. Some psychologists would place an ANTISOCIAL PERSONALITY in this category.

Charcot, Jean-Martin (1825–1893) French physician and early PSYCHOTHERAPIST whose use of HYPNOSIS to reach the depth of his patients' problems led him to the conclusion that all NEUROSIS had sexual roots. However he bowed to his Victorian ethos and never made this conclusion public. One of his students, SIGMUND FREUD, as well as adopting his teacher's methods and conclusions, did have the courage of his convictions and made his beliefs public. Freud was, however, sufficiently impressed by Charcot to name one of his children after him.

charisma An elusive quality of PERSONALITY, often defined as 'personal magnetism', which is considered by some SOCIAL SCIENTISTS to be an essential element in leadership.

childhood Usually defined as the period of human development between birth (or sometimes infancy) and puberty, at around 12 years of age, ie, a biological definition. Marking this period off from every other, treating people differently during it and expecting different behaviour from them, gives it a particular

PSYCHOLOGICAL importance. In this sense childhood is not a universal PHENOMENON. It varies culturally and historically, and in some societies does not even appear to exist. See AGEISM.

Children's Apperception Test A version of the THEMATIC APPERCEPTION TEST adapted for children.

chi square A simple statistical test (χ^2) widely used in PSYCHOLOGY to see whether observed results differ from those expected by chance alone.

chromosomes The parts of a cell nucleus that carry the GENES.

chunking A way of grouping items of information into units or chunks as an aid to memorising them.

clairvoyance The ability to see or perceive things without the use of the eyes or other sense organs. Ie a form of EXTRASENSORY PERCEPTION. See also PARAPSYCHOLOGY.

clang association A type of response to a WORD ASSOCIATION TEST which is based on similarity of sound, eg, 'master-faster'.

classical conditioning A simple form of learning by ASSOCIATION produced by an experimental procedure that PAVLOV developed in the early years of the 20th century. It involves the repeated pairing of a CONDITIONED STIMULUS (eg sound of a bell) with an UNCONDITIONED STIMULUS (eg food) thereby eliciting a CONDITIONED RESPONSE (salivation) to the conditioned stimulus (bell) which is similar to the UNCONDITIONED RESPONSE (salivation) previously elicited by the UNCONDITIONED STIMULUS (food).

claustrophobia A PHOBIA of confined spaces.

Clever Hans Name of a German horse reputed to have advanced skills in arithmetic. In fact Hans was responding cleverly to very subtle and UNCONSCIOUS cues from his trainer about when to start 'counting', by pawing the ground, and when to stop. Clever Hans is symptomatic of the ANTHROPOMORPHISM that has plagued the study of PSYCHOLOGY since man first began to domesticate animals and was struck by some of their apparently human responses. This PHENOMENON has become more complex with the ATTENTION being paid to the ROLE of language in thought. Some psychologists have been struck by the apparently human linguistic abilities of chimps. Though this claim is harder to disprove than the case of Clever Hans there is no clear evidence that chimps, or any other animals, have anything remotely approaching the linguistic and intellectual understanding or creativity of humans. See also EXPERIMENTER BIAS, ROSENTHAL

EFFECT, and SELF-FULFILLING PROPHECY, for other examples of the same kind of phenomenon.

client   Used of someone who seeks counselling or PSYCHO-THERAPY from a practitioner with a HUMANISTIC or NON-DIRECTIVE approach.

client-centred therapy   A form of PSYCHOTHERAPY developed by CARL ROGERS which is based on an unconditional acceptance and regard for the CLIENT. The client (as opposed to patient) is not diagnosed for any prescribed treatment but is encouraged to mobilize his own psychic resources to solve his own problems as he sees them. See also NON-DIRECTIVE THERAPY.

clinical psychologist   A practitioner of CLINICAL PSYCHOLOGY, usually with a PhD in the subject. Clinical psychologists may also be PSYCHOANALYSTS or other kinds of PSYCHOTHERAPISTS. They may work in hospitals or clinics or they may have a private practice. Compare with PSYCHIATRIST.

clinical psychology   The branch of PSYCHOLOGY concerned with the application of psychological theory and research to the diagnosis and treatment of emotional, mental, or behavioural disorders. Compare with PSYCHIATRY.

closure   A principle of GESTALT PSYCHOLOGY that has generally been accepted in the study of PERCEPTION; ie, that the BRAIN has a built-in tendency to perceive meaning, completion, and coherence where the OBJECTIVE sensory facts may have no meaning, be incomplete or incoherent. Thus a figure with a part missing will be perceived as though it were whole. The term is also used in PSYCHOTHERAPY (and even in general parlance) to denote a line of investigation that has been opened up but not yet completed.

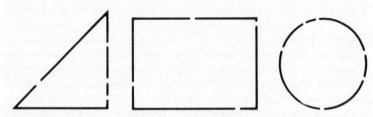

Figure 7   Closure

clustering   See CHUNKING.
cns   See CENTRAL NERVOUS SYSTEM.

coacting group   Sociological term for people who share the same goal but work towards it without communicating or interacting.

cocktail party phenomenon   Term used by some psychologists to describe our perceptual ability to deal with several messages at once but attend to only one of them.

cognition   A general term which includes all the psychological processes by which people become aware of, and gain knowledge about, the world.

cognitive dissonance   A kind of BALANCE THEORY proposed by the American psychologist Leon Festinger; the theory states that because we have a powerful DRIVE towards consistency (or consonance), if we hold two psychologically inconsistent COGNITIONS (beliefs, ATTITUDES, values or ideas) at the same time, or if our BEHAVIOUR clashes with those cognitions, we will be in an unpleasant state of tension which we are strongly motivated to reduce. As the theory deals with PSYCHOLOGICAL rather than logical inconsistency, it proposes that we are not so much concerned with actually being consistent as with feeling that we are consistent.

cognitive learning theory   A school of thought in PSYCHOLOGY which opposed the behaviourist view that there is a direct link between stimulus and response via the nervous system, arguing that complex learning involves the restructuring and reorganizing of knowledge and ideas by the BRAIN. Contrast with BEHAVIOURISM.

cognitive map   According to the American learning theorist, E C Tolman, a mental representation by an animal or human of the way in which a goal can be achieved or a problem solved. From his work on rats Tolman came to believe that the animals learned a cognitive map of the MAZE and not simply a series of movements.

cognitive overload   A situation in which someone is receiving more information than he can process.

cold emotion   A physiological state resulting from the injection of ADRENALIN. The bodily changes that occur resemble those associated with an emotional experience, but the subjects report feeling that they should be having an emotional experience without actually doing so. Ie, they feel tense or excited without knowing why.

collective mind   The idea that there are mental attributes of a group over and above those of the individuals composing it.

Alternatively, the idea that a group shares common mental processes that leads it to take concerted action.

collective unconscious   A central concept of JUNGIAN psychology which refers to the part of a person's UNCONSCIOUS that he shares with every other human being and which is inherited from previous generations in the distant past. Jung had been impressed by the similarities he saw between the symbolism of DREAMS and the artistic imagery of widely separated times and places. Most non-Jungians regard the concept as mystical.

colour blindness   An inability to distinguish colours that may be total or partial. Total colour blindness is very rare but partial colour blindness (particularly the inability to distinguish red and green from each other or from grey) is surprisingly common. It has been estimated that about eight to ten per cent of males are born with this defect, though it is rare in women.

colour constancy   The tendency for objects to be perceived as the same colour even when the light illuminating them changes colour.

colour contrast   The tendency for the difference between two colours to be intensified when they are placed side by side.

colour vision   The process by which the eye discriminates between different wave lengths of light, thus providing the BRAIN with the information necessary to perceive what we describe as colours.

combat fatigue   See BATTLE FATIGUE.

communicator credibility   In SOCIAL PSYCHOLOGY the extent to which the communicator of a message is believable. Thought to be related to whether the communicator is perceived as expert and trustworthy or not.

community psychology   A combination of applied CLINICAL and SOCIAL PSYCHOLOGY that attempts to foster the well-being of psychologically disturbed people by intervening in their social environment and utilizing the resources of their community to help them adapt.

comparative psychology   The branch of PSYCHOLOGY that compares different species, including humans, and attempts to understand the similarities and differences in their mental and behavioural lives.

compensation   As used in PSYCHOANALYSIS, this is a DEFENCE MECHANISM in which a person perceives himself to be lacking in some way and tries to make up for it by substituting some other characteristic which is perhaps exaggerated. This was a key concept in the work of ALFRED ADLER who suggested that, in this way, a small man might compensate for his lack of size by being aggressive and dominating psychologically. See INFERIORITY COMPLEX.

completion test   Name given to a mental test that requires the subject to fill in the missing letter, word, or phrase. First devised by the German psychologist Ebbinghaus in the late 19th century.

complex   In PSYCHOANALYSIS, a group of REPRESSED emotionally charged ideas that conflict with other ideas (representing other aspects of the PERSONALITY) that the individual is CONSCIOUS of.

compliance   In SOCIAL PSYCHOLOGY, a form of yielding to group pressure where there is a change in behaviour but without any underlying change of ATTITUDE.

compulsion   An overwhelming UNCONSCIOUS need to engage in some BEHAVIOUR that is usually contrary to one's CONSCIOUS WISHES. Compare with OBSESSION.

computer assisted instruction   A method of PROGRAMMED LEARNING in which a computer is used as a TEACHING MACHINE.

conation   A vague term used to denote a general PSYCHOLOGICAL activity variously described as impulse, desire, will, and striving. Formerly used along with AFFECTION and COGNITION as a tripartite division of psychological life.

concept formation   A particularly human form of mental ability that seems to be closely associated with the use of language. It involves the BRAIN in abstracting the essential qualities of individual things and classifying them by higher order rules or groups.

concrete operations   The level of cognitive ability attained in the third of PIAGET's stages of development from about 7 to 11 years of age. At this stage children are supposed to be capable of logical thinking about concrete objects, while abstract thinking is still beyond them. The most important achievement of this stage is the idea of CONSERVATION.

concrete thinking   Thinking that is rigidly confined to the experiences of the moment. Often due to BRAIN DAMAGE. Sometimes used in the more general sense of thinking in concrete rather than abstract terms because it is easier, or being unable to see the wood for the trees.

conditioned response   A response resulting solely from the process of CONDITIONING. See also CLASSICAL CONDITIONING and PAVLOV.

conditioned stimulus A stimulus that is originally ineffective in eliciting a given response but becomes effective after a process of CONDITIONING. See also CLASSICAL CONDITIONING and PAVLOV.

conditioning A process of learning in humans or animals, via an experimental procedure, where a given stimulus produces a response other than its normal, natural, or automatic one. In the CLASSICAL form developed by PAVLOV a dog learned to salivate at the sound of a bell or buzzer and not just at the presentation of food. Later B F SKINNER developed a different procedure known as OPERANT CONDITIONING in which an animal's simple response could be used as the basis for training it to engage in very complex behaviour.

confabulation Filling in blanks in the memory with plausible stories that are untrue but not deliberate lies. Occurs in people whose memory is disturbed through BRAIN DAMAGE and who don't realise that their stories are confabulations.

congenital Something that is present in an individual at birth but is not necessarily INNATE.

conscious Being aware of the environment. In PSYCHOANALYSIS, those aspects of one's psychological functioning of which the EGO is aware.

consciousness The AWARENESS of oneself in every aspect of one's being.

consensual validation Checking one's PERCEPTIONS of something with other people as a way of knowing whether what is perceived is real or illusory.

conservation In the work of PIAGET this is the most important achievement in the stage of CONCRETE OPERATIONS (7–11 years). Children learn that an object stays the same (is conserved) even while its appearance changes. Thus they understand for the first time that when water is transferred from a tall thin glass to a short fat one, the amount of water remains constant. (Fig. 8)

consolidation The idea that after something has been learned physiological changes take place in the BRAIN that help fix it in the memory.

constant object of love According to the American PSYCHO-ANALYST Margaret Mahler, a form of emotional OBJECT CONSTANCY where the mother is perceived as the constant object of love.

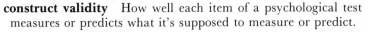

Figure 8 Conservation

construct validity   How well each item of a psychological test measures or predicts what it's supposed to measure or predict.

contagion theory of crowds   A modern variant in SOCIOLOGY of the old idea of GROUP MIND. In this version the effect of a crowd is to assimilate individuals within it, producing an overriding psychological unity and changing an individual's usual psychological responses in the process. Compare with COLLECTIVE MIND.

contamination   In EXPERIMENTAL PSYCHOLOGY, the distorting effect of uncontrolled factors external to the EXPERIMENT, the most important being the CONSCIOUS or UNCONSCIOUS assumptions of the experimenter. See EXPERIMENTER BIAS and ROSENTHAL EFFECT.

content analysis   The analysis of material in PSYCHOLOGY and in SOCIAL SCIENCE to see what categories or themes emerge, or the analysis of material by prearranged theme or categories to test a HYPOTHESIS or make a diagnosis.

contiguity   One of the LAWS OF ASSOCIATION first introduced in the fourth century BC by Aristotle. The idea that the BRAIN tends to associate stimuli which occur close together in time or space.

continuity   Similar to CONTIGUITY and associated with GESTALT PSYCHOLOGY. The idea that the BRAIN will perceive stimuli as belonging with each other and forming a pattern if they follow each other closely and regularly in time or space.

contour   The outline or boundary of an object, which is essential to its being perceived.

control group   In EXPERIMENTAL PSYCHOLOGY, a group of sub-

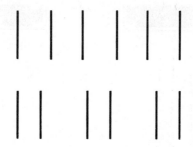

Figure 9 Contiguity. We see six single lines on top, but three pairs of lines below.

jects as similar as possible to the EXPERIMENTAL GROUP for purposes of comparison. They share the same conditions of the experimental group except exposure to the EXPERIMENTAL VARIABLE which is the object of the study.

conventional stage According to the American psychologist Laurence Kohlberg, the second of three broad levels of moral development – beyond which most people do not mature. At this level people judge the rightness or wrongness of an action in terms of what other people think and the dictates of authority. See STAGE THEORIES.

convergent thinking Thinking along conventional lines in an attempt to find the best single answer to a problem. Compare with DIVERGENT THINKING.

conversion hysteria The kind of HYSTERIA, especially common in the early days of PSYCHOANALYSIS, which converts psychological conflict into the form of serious physical problems like paralysis. Such striking PHENOMENA are now rare (perhaps because of increased sophistication about UNCONSCIOUS dynamics) though SOMATISING and PSYCHOSOMATIC illnesses are still with us.

correlation The relationship or DEPENDENCE between two VARIABLES.

correlation coefficient A statistic (r) that measures the extent to which two VARIABLES are correlated. It can range from zero correlation to perfect positive correlation (1.00), where the variables are always associated in the same way, or perfect negative correlation (−1.00), where the variables are always associated but in different ways.

co-twin control An experimetal procedure in which one IDENT-ICAL TWIN (the subject) is given a particular treatment while the other (the control) is not. Used in studies (like IQ or INTELLI-GENCE) where the effects of HEREDITY are of particular interest.

counterculture   A way of life which is deliberately opposed to and differentiated from the dominant way of life in a society.

counter-transference   In PSYCHOANALYSIS, the ANALYST'S TRANSFERENCE on to his patient. Often used more widely to describe the analyst's feelings towards the patient.

cretinism   Mental and physical retardation due to thyroid defi-ciency in early infancy.

criterion group   A group of people of known characteristics, achievement, or BEHAVIOUR who are used as a standard against which other people are compared in terms of scores on psycho-logical tests. See IQ and INTELLIGENCE TEST.

critical flicker frequency   The point at which a flickering light no longer appears to flicker but is perceived as a steady light. See FLICKER FUSION FREQUENCY.

critical period   A point of development at which a human or animal is thought to be optimally ready to learn certain skills or be open to certain influences. See IMPRINTING.

crowding behaviour   Supposed response of an animal or human to the effects of being crowded, and often subject to very dubious GENERALIZATION across species. For example, the aggressive behaviour of rats at a certain level of crowding is thought by many to be INSTINCTIVE, and this 'explanation' may then be offered to account for violence in urban slums. There is little hard evidence that any human behaviour is instinctive, and as an explanation for the extremely complex (and sometimes appar-ently contradictory) relationship between urban violence and crowding it is so simplistic as to be silly.

cultural determinism   The viewpoint that the dominant influ-ences in the development of PERSONALITY, and the occurrence of particular behaviour patterns, are cultural rather than geneti-cally inherited. See also CULTURE.

cultural lag   The continued use of outmoded ways of doing things even after the introduction of more effective means for attaining the particular goals of a society. A social version of DECENTRING.

cultural relativism   The viewpoint that judgments of different ways of life or definitions of universal human interests (like truth, beauty, and goodness) can never be made in absolute terms but only within the context of a given CULTURE.

culture In the anthropological sense a culture is usually defined as the shared beliefs, values, ATTITUDES, and expectations about appropriate ways to behave, that are held by the members of a social group. To a psychologist the unquestioned assumptions people share about the world, about the human condition, about what is right, wrong, and NORMAL, are perhaps even more important.

culture-free tests Psychological tests from which the influences or advantages of particular cultural experiences have been eliminated. Such tests could therefore be given to anyone anywhere with equal VALIDITY, and when someone invents one you'll be the first to know about it.

curiosity The tendency among humans and animals to explore their environment for its own sake.

curve of forgetting A graphic representation of the rate at which forgetting occurs.

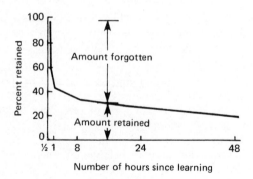

Figure 10 Curve of forgetting
(from *Principles of General Psychology*, 4th edition, G A Kimble, N Ganvegy and E Zigler, New York, Ronald Press, 1974, p 417)

curvilinear relationship A relationship between two VARIABLES depicted graphically by a curve rather than a straight line. (Fig. 11)

cybernetics A Greek term meaning something like 'steersman', introduced in 1948 by Norbert Wiener, a computer engineer. It is usually defined briefly as the study of regulatory mechanisms (like thermostats). Out of this field came the analogy of the BRAIN as a computer and the model of psychological processes as systems of messages with their own built-in FEEDBACK.

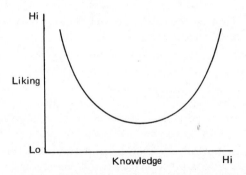

Figure 11   Curvilinear relationship. Illustration of the hypothesis that one's liking for someone or something may not increase directly (in a linear fashion) with increased knowledge, but may start off high under first impressions, decline with limited information and increase again with increased knowledge.

D

dancing mania   A MANIA that takes the form of wild, uncontrollable dancing. First noticed in the 14th century as an epidemic that raged across Europe in the wake of the Black Death or bubonic plague, apparently as a result of mass religious frenzy combined with some damage to the nervous system from the disease.

dark adaptation   The process by which the eye adjusts to lowered illumination.

Darwin, Charles (1809–1882)   English biologist who presented systematic evidence for the inevitability of EVOLUTION and the theory that it is accomplished by a process of NATURAL SELECTION. See also SOCIAL DARWINISM.

Darwinian reflex   A grasping reflex found only in very young animal or human infants.

David's Dictum   In any given place, at any given time, people are never where they're supposed to be.

death instinct   According to FREUD, an UNCONSCIOUS DRIVE towards constriction of the PERSONALITY, destructiveness, and death. Always contrasted with the LIFE INSTINCT. Taken most seriously by followers of Melanie Klein.

decentring   Continuing to perceive a situation in a way that changing circumstances have rendered ineffective. A psychological version of CULTURAL LAG.

decortication Surgical removal of the CEREBRAL CORTEX.

defence mechanism FREUD's term for the ways in which the EGO protects itself from threatening UNCONSCIOUS ideas of the ID or the SUPEREGO, or from external dangers in the environment. See also DENIAL, PROJECTION, RATIONALIZATION, REACTION-FORMATION, REGRESSION, REPRESSION, SUBLIMATION and UNDOING.

defensive attribution A concept important in both CLINICAL and SOCIAL PSYCHOLOGY which refers to the tendency to blame the victim of a frightening misfortune as a way of avoiding the ANXIETY-provoking thought that one could be in the victim's place. For example, 'rape victims ask for it.'

definition of the situation In SOCIOLOGY this refers to the way someone perceives and interprets the nature of the SOCIAL INTERACTION in which he or she participates; associated with the dictum of the American sociologist W I Thomas that 'if human beings define situations as real, they are real in their consequences.'

dehumanization The process of treating other people as something other than human. Often done out of fear and with the purpose of reducing GUILT about aggressive behaviour. See DIABOLISM.

deindividuation Feelings of anonymity and being part of a crowd. A blurring of individual IDENTITY and a loosening of INHIBITIONS. See COLLECTIVE MIND and CONTAGION THEORY OF CROWDS.

déjà vu literally, 'already seen'. The ILLUSION of recognising something although it is a new experience. Perhaps due to a disturbance of the BRAIN's memory functions.

delayed gratification Sociological term for the act of foregoing present satisfaction for the sake of greater satisfaction some time in the future. For example, saving money rather than spending it. Supposed to be more typical of the middle classes than any other group in our society.

delirium An ALTERED STATE OF CONSCIOUSNESS characterized by DELUSIONS, HALLUCINATIONS, and ILLUSIONS.

delirium tremens A DELIRIUM suffered by chronic alcoholics after withdrawal of alcohol.

delta waves Large, slow BRAIN WAVES, about three a second. Found only in deep sleep.

delusion   A false belief that is impervious to evidence or reason. Often a symptom of PSYCHOSIS.

delusions of grandeur   The DELUSION that one is a celebrated or exalted person.

delusions of persecution   An individual's DELUSION that his problems are caused by other people conspiring against him.

demand characteristics   In EXPERIMENTAL PSYCHOLOGY, the CONSCIOUS or UNCONSCIOUS cues which reveal an experimenter's expectations of his subject's behaviour. Subjects tend to react by trying to meet these expectations, to deny them or to present themselves in a favourable light. See also EXPERIMENTER BIAS.

denial   The DEFENCE MECHANISM whereby someone refuses to accept either the occurrence of a painful experience or the existence of an ANXIETY-provoking impulse.

dependence   Used in at least three senses (and sometimes written 'dependency'). **1** In science generally, if one thing is caused by another it is said to be dependent on it. **2** In CLINICAL PSYCHOLOGY a person is said to be dependent on someone or something to the extent that he needs that thing or person in order to go about his regular activities. **3** In SOCIAL PSYCHOLOGY it is sometimes used to refer to the way in which people in a group rely on each other for a definition of reality.

dependent variable   In EXPERIMENTAL PSYCHOLOGY, the VARIABLE whose state is one of DEPENDENCE on the INDEPENDENT VARIABLE. The independent variable constitutes the stimulus and the dependent variable the response. Any changes measured in the response are attributed to the effects of the stimulus.

depression   One of the most common forms of emotional disturbance which can vary in intensity from an everyday attack of 'the blues' to a PSYCHOTIC condition of paralysing hopelessness. It is characterized by ANXIETY, dejection, and a general lowering of activity. There is a difference of opinion as to whether (or to what extent) the causes of depression are to be found in UNCONSCIOUS conflict or in biochemical malfunctioning of the BRAIN.

deprivation   The lack of something considered essential to psychological well-being. See MATERNAL, SENSORY, and SOCIAL deprivation.

depth interview   A situation in which the interviewer tries to get beyond the CONSCIOUS responses of the interviewee to probe UNCONSCIOUS feelings.

depth perception   The AWARENESS of how distant objects are from the eye, and the ability to PERCEIVE the world as three dimensional, ie as having depth as well as height and width.

depth psychology   The study of the part the UNCONSCIOUS plays in human behaviour. See also DYNAMIC PSYCHOLOGY.

descriptive statistics   STATISTICS that summarize or describe a set of measurements, eg MEASURES OF CENTRAL TENDENCY. Compare with INFERENTIAL STATISTICS.

desensitization   Decreased sensitivity to an aspect of PERSONALITY one had previously considered undesirable. Often a form of BEHAVIOUR THERAPY that associates threatening stimuli with relaxation rather than fear.

determinism   The PHILOSOPHY that nothing happens without a cause and everything that happens is the necessary result of previous conditions. Given complete knowledge of previous conditions one would fully understand any given behaviour.

developmental psychology   The branch of PSYCHOLOGY that deals with the interactions of physical, psychological, and social changes that occur as an individual increases in age. For a long time this meant largely CHILDHOOD development and perhaps ADOLESCENCE, but increasing attention is now being paid to MIDDLESCENCE and SENESCENCE.

developmental tasks   Skills and achievements that are considered necessary for children to attain at certain ages to ensure their psychological well-being, eg, walking, talking, reading.

deviate   Someone whose behaviour violates prevailing NORMS of morality in his society.

deviation   A departure from the NORM. In STATISTICS, the difference of a given score from the MEAN.

diabolism   Attributing to a person or group the attributes of the devil. A process of DEHUMANIZATION frequently encountered in wartime where there is a powerful need to assuage ANXIETY and GUILT by making the enemy all bad and one's own side all good.

diagnostic test   An instrument used by psychologists for probing the nature of a mental or emotional difficulty. See PROJECTIVE TECHNIQUES.

diathermy   A form of SHOCK TREATMENT for severe psychological disturbance using electrical current to raise the temperature of the blood.

difference limen   See JUST NOTICEABLE DIFFERENCE.

differential threshold   See JUST NOTICEABLE DIFFERENCE.

differentiation In CONDITIONING, a procedure whereby an animal is trained to distinguish between two similar stimuli or two similar responses.

diffusion of responsibility In SOCIAL PSYCHOLOGY, the suggestion that taking responsibility for initiating action or offering help in an emergency is spread among the people present in the situation. Sometimes the responsibility is so diffuse that no action is taken. See BYSTANDER APATHY. The term can also be more generally used about the diffusion of decision making responsibility in the presence of other people.

digit-span test A way of testing a person's MEMORY SPAN by asking her to recall a series of random numbers or digits after a single hearing. Most people can recall seven digits, on average.

diminishing returns An idea borrowed from economics to describe an improvement that gets progressively smaller with each succeeding increment. In PSYCHOLOGY it is used in the study of learning and memory where after a large gain at the beginning, extra practice begins to provide less and less gain.

Dionysian Anthropological concept borrowed from ancient Greece where Dionysus, the god of wine and physical pleasure, represented the primitive, impulsive, and emotional aspects of the human condition. Contrasted with APOLLONIAN.

dipsomania A MANIA that takes the form of a periodic craving for alcohol. Unlike chronic alcoholism the patient is not DEPENDENT on a daily intake of alcohol, and his bouts of drinking are thought to be symptomatic of a deep-lying emotional disorder.

discrimination In PSYCHOLOGY this is simply the ability to perceive differences. In a social or political context 'difference' comes to signify something to be feared and rejected.

disinhibition A PHENOMENON discovered in CLASSICAL CONDITIONING. If an animal is conditioned to salivate at a certain stimulus and is then rewarded with food, when the food reward is withdrawn, its CONDITIONED RESPONSE will be inhibited and it will stop salivating. But if a different stimulus is suddenly used the animal will start salivating again (as though the INHIBITION were itself being inhibited).

disintegration Literally, the loss of INTEGRATION or organization of something whose parts usually fit together harmoniously. In PSYCHOLOGY it is used most often about PERSONALITY whose thinking, feeling, and acting components can disintegrate under the STRESS of severe psychological disturbance. See also PSYCHOSIS.

displacement In PSYCHOANALYSIS, the UNCONSCIOUS shifting of feeling from its real object to another where it is less threatening to the EGO. For example, shouting at the television set rather than arguing with the boss. This is why symbols are considered important in DREAMS. See also DREAM WISH and DREAM WORK.

display In ETHOLOGY, the concept that a male animal will show itself off to best advantage either to fight or woo when it is approached by the appropriate stimulus of a male or female of the same species. The concept is often applied to human adolescent behaviour.

display rules Sometimes used in SOCIOLOGY to indicate BEHAVIOUR designed to mask real feelings by presenting what appears to be a different feeling.

dissociation A situation in which a set of integrated psychological processes split off from the rest of an individual's PERSONALITY and appear to take on an independent existence of their own. See AMNESIA and the basis for MULTIPLE PERSONALITY.

distributed practice A technique of learning in which the lessons or periods of practice are spread out as widely as the available time permits. A much more effective method of learning than MASSED PRACTICE with which it is usually contrasted.

distribution Statistical term for the arrangement of data in categories and their display in the form of a graph or table.

distributive justice A situation in which everyone receives a just reward. Even though this situation rarely occurs in real life, it has been suggested that people need to operate on the basis of a JUST-WORLD HYPOTHESIS.

divergent thinking Creative and original thinking that deviates from the obvious and the conventional to produce several possible solutions to a particular problem. Contrasted with CONVERGENT THINKING.

dizygotic twins Commonly known as FRATERNAL TWINS. Twins who develop from two separate fertilized eggs, or ZYGOTES. They are therefore not identical, may be of different sexes, and have no more in common genetically than any other siblings. Contrast with MONOZYGOTIC TWINS.

dominance Used of a person with a strong need to control, or be more important than, other people. See also DOMINANT GENE and CEREBRAL DOMINANCE.

dominant gene The appearance in an offspring of a certain physical characteristic as a result of one factor dominating the other it is paired with in a parental GENE. See RECESSIVE GENE.

Doppler effect The increase or decrease in light waves or sound waves as the source of the light or sound approaches or recedes from an observer. For example, the whistle of a train as it rushes past is perceived as changing its pitch.

double-bind theory The view that contradictory messages or conflicting demands can induce severe STRESS and even SCHIZOPHRENIA in an individual. Used especially of a DEPENDENT relationship such as that between child and parent where the child can neither resolve nor escape the psychological dilemmas of the situation. See also EXPERIMENTAL NEUROSIS.

double-blind technique An experimental method in which neither the subject nor the experimenter is aware of the point at which the experimental manipulation is introduced. Used especially of EXPERIMENTS with drugs where neither subject nor experimenter knows which drug is being administered when and to whom. The technique is an attempt to overcome the CONSCIOUS and UNCONSCIOUS effects of EXPERIMENTER BIAS.

Down's syndrome A form of CONGENITAL mental retardation which is due to a genetic abnormality. It is accompanied by certain facial characteristics, popularly thought to be Asiatic, hence also the term mongolism. Apparently Down's syndrome occurs most frequently in children of older mothers.

Draw-a-person Test A PROJECTIVE TECHNIQUE in which young children are asked to draw a person as a gross test of intellectual ability, or mental retardation. It is also used in research on the SELF CONCEPT.

dream Imagery that occurs during sleep, usually with a certain coherence but sometimes with bizarre, unusual, or confusing aspects as well.

dream interpretation A basic technique of PSYCHOANALYSIS where the FREE ASSOCIATION of the patient to the various elements of his DREAMS is employed in an attempt to understand their hidden meaning. FREUD regarded dreams as 'the royal road to the unconscious', and as no activity of the UNCONSCIOUS is random or meaningless the symbolism to be found in a dream represented an important clue to the patient's underlying MOTIVATION. See also LATENT CONTENT and MANIFEST CONTENT.

dream research In the 1950s it was discovered that RAPID EYE

MOVEMENTS (REMs) were associated with dreaming, thus providing a possibility for studying the biological functions of DREAMS experimentally. This experimental work appears to support FREUD's contention that dreams are an essential part of psychological functioning. When people are awakened during REM sleep and thus deprived of their dreams, they seem to experience signs of psychological disturbance. Where Freud asserted that the dream functions to keep the dreamer asleep by transforming his unacceptable wishes into a more comfortable form, some experimenters would argue that the reverse is more nearly true, that the function of sleep is actually to allow one to dream. Many people can function well on very little sleep but all human beings (and even higher animals) appear to have a biological need to dream when they are asleep.

dream wish In PSYCHOANALYSIS, the form in which a repressed wish appears in a dream. See WISH FULFILMENT.

dream work In PSYCHOANALYSIS, the process by which the desires of the ID are converted in the UNCONSCIOUS into acceptable material for DREAMS.

drive A general term for a strong urge in an animal or human, including those urges that are sometimes referred to as instinctive. See INSTINCT and MOTIVATION.

drive reduction The weakening of a DRIVE in an animal or human, usually as a result of the appropriate needs being satisfied.

DTs See DELIRIUM TREMENS.

dual personality A special case of MULTIPLE PERSONALITY.

dyad The sociological way of referring to two people.

dynamic psychology Those aspects of PSYCHOLOGY that are concerned with MOTIVATION and with understanding the underlying causes of behaviour in all its ramifications. PSYCHOANALYSIS and psychoanalytically influenced areas of psychology are the prime, but not the only, examples of dynamic psychology: GESTALT PSYCHOLOGY would also qualify, for instance.

dyslexia An impairment of word PERCEPTION involving a loss of ability to read or understand words. Contrast with ALEXIA.

E

echolalia The meaningless and involuntary repetition of words or phrases that someone else has just said. Usually a sign of PSYCHOSIS or serious BRAIN DAMAGE.

echolocation A technique for locating objects in the environment by emitting sound waves and then perceiving them as they reflect back off the objects. This technique, which is the basis of sonar systems for detecting objects in the water, has been learned from the behaviour of whales and bats. Blind people use it, often without realising it, when they tap their sticks on walls or floors. The echoes they hear allow them to locate objects around them.

ECT See ELECTRO-CONVULSIVE THERAPY.

educational psychology The branch of PSYCHOLOGY that deals with the principles and methods of training and of education in general.

EEG See ELECTROENCEPHALOGRAPH.

effective stimulus A stimulus that produces a response when applied to an appropriate sense receptor. For example, shining a light in front of a subject's eye would probably be an effective stimulus; shining it at the subject's back would probably not.

efferent The process of transmitting nervous impulses from the BRAIN through the nervous system to the glands and muscles. Contrast with AFFERENT.

efficacy A term sometimes used in SOCIAL PSYCHOLOGY to indicate how effective a person feels in influencing matters of importance to her.

ego literally, the 'I', the CONSCIOUS AWARENESS of oneself (one's SELF). According to FREUD the ego is that part of the PERSONALITY closest to external reality which holds the ring between the UNCONSCIOUS drives of the pleasure seeking ID on the one hand and the internalized restrictions of the SUPEREGO, on the other. NEUROSIS in Freud's view is thus the result of the ego being unable to maintain harmonious relations with the id and superego because the power of their unconscious DRIVES are too much for it to cope with.

egocentricity Literally, 'self-centred', an interest in oneself to the point of excluding any interest in other people. In PIAGET's theory of development the term does not have any pejorative connotation of selfishness but refers to a STAGE, that lasts till the age of seven or eight, where a child is unable to adopt someone else's perceptual frame of reference and see a situation through his eyes. Thus a child at this stage is unable to describe what an object looks like to someone sitting across the table from him – he describes it the way it appears to him. The child's conceptual, cognitive world is similarly egocentric. A 'foreigner', for instance, is always a foreigner, even in his own country, but the child himself is never a foreigner, even in someone else's country. This stage ends when the child achieves RECIPROCITY, though egocentric behaviour can often be observed in adults.

ego defence See DEFENCE MECHANISMS.

ego ideal In PSYCHOANALYSIS, a part of the SUPEREGO that represents an IDENTIFICATION with parents or parent figures who are admired and loved.

ego psychology An emphasis found in post-Freudian PSYCHO-ANALYTIC theory which gives more importance to the functions of the EGO and its relations to external reality than FREUD had done.

ego strength The ability of an individual to maintain the EGO in its function of avoiding emotional disturbance and maladjustment.

eidetic imagery Commonly known as photographic memory. Exceptionally vivid (usually visual) imagery of objects or events that have previously been experienced. The images are as clear as if the subject were perceiving them still. The ability to experience eidetic imagery is common, if not universal, in young children, but in most people it disappears with age.

elaborated code British psychologist Basil Bernstein's term for an articulate style of communication in which whole phrases are used to convey a precise and complex range of ideas and in which emotional and intellectual aspects are clearly differentiated. Said to be typical of the way middle-class parents interact with their children. Contrasted with RESTRICTED CODE.

Electra complex In FREUDIAN THEORY the Electra complex in females is analagous to the OEDIPUS COMPLEX in males. It refers to the UNCONSCIOUS desire that all daughters are supposed to have for sexual relations with their fathers.

electro-convulsive therapy A technique, used mainly in treating severe DEPRESSION, of producing behavioural changes by passing an electrical current briefly through a patient's BRAIN. The technique causes muscular convulsions and renders the patient unconscious. It is claimed that the patient's depression can often be eased in this way, but nobody knows why – nor whether there are any permanent long-term side effects. Nowadays the patient is usually given a sedative and a muscle relaxing drug before ECT to reduce the dangers of physical damage occurring. Commonly known as shock treatment.

electroencephalograph A machine for recording the continuous electrical activity of the BRAIN, usually through electrodes attached to the scalp. This activity is recorded on paper as BRAIN WAVES of different FREQUENCY.

embedded figure A figure concealed within a more complex figure. Once detected it is impossible to ignore.

Find this figure in this one

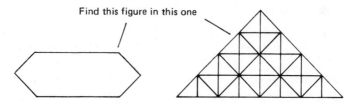

Figure 12 Embedded figure
(from *Principles of General Psychology*, 4th edition, G A Kimble, N Ganvegy and E Zigler, New York, Ronald Press, 1974, p 201)

emotion In the way psychologists use this term there is widespread agreement that it represents a complex state of diffuse physical changes, marked by strong feelings, and accompanied by a behavioural impulse towards achieving a specific goal. The IDENTIFICATION and labelling of particular emotions involves a large element of social learning and varies widely across time and place.

empathy The ability to understand someone else's feelings, though without actually feeling what he feels. It is regarded as an intellectual rather than an emotional experience. Compare with SYMPATHY.

empirical Based on experience or observation; the basis for experimental science.

empiricism The philosophy that personal experience is the only source of true knowledge. In PSYCHOLOGY it has the particular meaning, in problems such as the PERCEPTION of space, of an ability that is learned through experience rather than inherited genetically.

encephalitis An inflammation of the BRAIN, usually through an infectious disease. Sometimes results in PERSONALITY changes, including what appears to be a lowering of INTELLIGENCE.

encounter group See SENSITIVITY TRAINING.

endogamy The practice of restricting marriage partners to a person from one's own social or kinship group. Contrasted with EXOGAMY.

engineering psychology An American term for ERGONOMICS.

engram A hypothetical memory trace, or physical representation of memory. Many psychologists have long assumed that the process of learning and remembering results in some physical changes in BRAIN tissue, though no one has actually observed these changes.

enuresis Involuntary release of urine, such as bed-wetting in children, usually from emotional disturbance rather than organic causes.

environmental-stress theory A sociological interpretation of what psychologists would refer to as NEUROSIS, which is attributed to the distorting effect of a given environment on behaviour tendencies common to everyone.

epigenesis A biological theory about the development of the embryo which stresses the influence of the environment. The interaction of embryo and environment produces new properties that were not present in the fertilized egg, or ZYGOTE. In certain psychological theories, especially those of ERIK ERIKSON, epigenesis refers to a sequence of developmental stages that must be followed to attain psychological maturity.

epilepsy Disturbances in the electrical activity of the BRAIN caused by a neurological disorder. In the severe form, or GRAND MAL, the patient may suffer violent convulsions and prolonged loss of CONSCIOUSNESS. In the mild form, or PETIT MAL, the seizure may produce only a momentary dizziness or loss of consciousness. Anticonvulsant drugs can often control the grand mal seizures, but the causes of epilepsy, a disease known for thousands of years as the 'falling sickness', are still unknown.

epinephrine See ADRENALIN.

epiphenomenalism The philosophical doctrine that mental activities have no separate existence apart from the body, but are simply by-products of the BRAIN's processes.

epiphenomenon In the philosophy of MIND, an event that accompanies another event without having any causal relationship to it.

epistemology The branch of PHILOSOPHY that deals with the search for true knowledge; the origins, nature, limits and verifiability of what is known.

equal-status contact Like it says. Considered essential by SOCIAL SCIENTISTS in breaking down social prejudices. Mere contact apparently just intensifies pre-existing PREJUDICES.

ergonomics The study of people at work, and in particular their relationship to machines.

Erikson, Erik (born 1902) A PSYCHOANALYST who is usually classified as a neo-Freudian because of his emphasis on EGO PSYCHOLOGY. Erikson has an overriding interest in problems of IDENTITY. In his book *Childhood and Society*, he proposes the principle of EPIGENESIS, that there is a sequence of eight stages of development, all of them with crucial psychological tasks to be achieved and through each of which an individual must successfully pass in order to attain maturity. The most crucial of these periods is that of ADOLESCENCE, when the individual is in the process of forming an identity through the activity of his EGO or conscious SELF.

Erikson's concern with identity crises led him to examine those of various historical figures, and his *Young Man Luther* generated a lot of interest in the field of PSYCHOHISTORY and in particular PSYCHOBIOGRAPHY. In general, Erikson has influenced numerous workers in the field of human development to discount the exclusive Freudian focus on CHILDHOOD and pay more serious attention to adolescence – and, to a lesser extent, the entire life cycle.

erogenous zones Areas of the body whose stimulation are particularly prone to result in sexual arousal. The all-time favourites would appear to be genitals, mouth and breasts, but this may be partly because they've had a better press (as it were) than other parts.

Eros The Greek god of love, used by FREUD to symbolise the LIBIDO or self-preserving drive for life. Contrasted with THANATOS.

ESP See EXTRASENSORY PERCEPTION.

estrogen See OESTROGEN.

ethnocentrism The tendency to regard the group one identifies with, especially one's ethnic group, as superior to any other. Like

EGOCENTRICITY in individuals it involves the inability to step outside the perceptual framework of one's own group and see life from the viewpoint of a different group.

ethnography The study of the history, customs, myths, traditions and CULTURE of ethnic groups. Such groups may have in common the same GENE pool, nationality, religion, language or any permutation of these factors.

ethnology The attempt to analyse and understand the ethnic group patterns of behaviour described by ETHNOGRAPHY.

ethnomethodology Associated with the American sociologist Harold Garfinkel; the attempt to focus on people's daily lives and examine their unquestioned assumptions about the social world.

ethology Formerly the study of ethical systems but more recently the comparative study of animal BEHAVIOUR in its natural habitat, especially the INNATE behaviours that appear irrespective of an animal's previous experiences.

etiology See AETIOLOGY.

eugenics A branch of applied GENETICS which attempts to improve the inherited qualities of a species by selective breeding. When the species concerned is homo sapiens the goals, values, criteria, and methods of eugenics immediately become ethical questions – which have been debated since Plato first proposed them in the fourth century BC.

euthanasia The practice of 'mercy killing', terminating a pain-filled life with a painless death.

evoked potential An electrical discharge in the BRAIN produced by the stimulation of a sense organ.

evolution A gradual process of genetic development and change in animal life over many generations. Those members of a species best adapted to their environment in any generation (ie, the 'fittest') have the best chance of surviving and reproducing successfully. See DARWIN, NATURAL SELECTION, and SURVIVAL VALUE.

exchange theory A way of explaining the relationship between two people in a DYAD. It is mainly concerned with examining the relative rewards and costs of the relationship for each individual. The theory was introduced to SOCIAL PSYCHOLOGY by John Thibout and Harold Kelley, and to SOCIOLOGY by George Homans.

exchange theory of friendship A sociological concept of friendship using the economic terminology of the market place, where people estimate their 'worth' and look for people of equal or greater worth to exchange friendship with. See EXCHANGE THEORY.

exhibitionism   A COMPULSION to expose oneself in public, either literally or metaphorically.

existential psychiatry   A movement that rejects the MEDICAL MODEL for the treatment of mental illness in favour of trying to analyse the CONSCIOUS SELF of the disturbed individual. Such a person is not treated as a patient to be cured but rather as an individual to be understood and to be helped in achieving self-understanding. See also LAING.

existential psychology   A movement or school that views the task of PSYCHOLOGY as an understanding of CONSCIOUSNESS and the contents of the MIND. The basic method of this school is INTROSPECTION, the concentration on immediate AWARENESS. This is a new and growing emphasis in psychology, dating no further back than WILHELM WUNDT in the 19th century.

exogamy   The practice of restricting marriage partners to a person from outside one's own social or kinship group. Contrasted with ENDOGAMY.

experiment   Observation of a given PHENOMENON under controlled conditions designed to isolate the cause of that phenomenon.

experimental design   Technically, the investigation of the way in which the INDEPENDENT VARIABLE in an EXPERIMENT affects the DEPENDENT VARIABLE, but used generally for the whole procedure of an experiment, from the selection of subjects to the statistical analysis of the results.

experimental group   Subjects in an EXPERIMENT who are exposed to the EXPERIMENTAL VARIABLE and whose BEHAVIOUR is expected to be influenced by it. Contrasted with the CONTROL GROUP which is not exposed to the experimental variable.

experimental neurosis   Disturbed BEHAVIOUR of animals in an EXPERIMENT when they are faced with an impossible problem. This PHENOMENON was discovered by PAVLOV when he rewarded a dog with food for responding (by salivating) to a circle and then withheld the reward when the stimulus was an ellipse. Pavlov gradually made the two stimuli more and more alike. When the point was reached at which the dog could no longer discriminate the circle from the ellipse the animal lashed out in a frenzy of wild and random behaviour. Whether this behaviour can be equated with human NEUROSIS is a matter of long-standing dispute among psychologists.

experimental psychology The use of experimental methods to study psychological PHENOMENA.

experimental variable Technically the name given to the INDEPENDENT VARIABLE when it can be manipulated by an experimenter. In practice the terms are often used interchangeably.

experimenter bias The effects on an EXPERIMENT of the CONSCIOUS or UNCONSCIOUS attempts by the experimenter to influence the outcome in the direction he has predicted. An important and pervasive problem, as the outcome of virtually every published experiment is in the predicted direction. The ramifications of this phenomenon are much wider than the experimental situation. See also DEMAND CHARACTERISTICS, DOUBLE-BLIND TECHNIQUE, INTERVIEWER BIAS, ROSENTHAL EFFECT and SELF-FULFULLING PROPHECY.

extended family Defined differently for different societies but always includes more distant relations (both genetically and geographically) than the NUCLEAR FAMILY with which it is contrasted.

externalization Used in various ways that sometimes shade into each other, eg: regarding one's thoughts and feelings as being caused by some external agency; projecting one's thoughts and feelings on to the external world; seeing one's own mental processes as being outside one's own MIND (as in hallucination); the process that occurs throughout CHILDHOOD of separating off one's sense of SELF from the external world; EGO formation in Freudian terms.

extinction In EXPERIMENTAL PSYCHOLOGY, the weakening of a CONDITIONED RESPONSE. This is accomplished either by presenting the CONDITIONED STIMULUS without the UNCONDITIONED STIMULUS or by withholding REINFORCEMENT from the conditioned response.

extrapunitive Characteristically reacting to frustration by behaving aggressively towards the people or objects seen as causing the frustration. Contrast with INTROPUNITIVE.

extrasensory perception The ability to receive information about the world from sources other than the known senses. Whether or not such abilities exist is still a matter of great debate among psychologists. See CLAIRVOYANCE, PRECOGNITION, PSYCHOKINESIS, and TELEPATHY, all of which are regarded as branches of ESP by people interested in PARAPSYCHOLOGY.

extraversion According to JUNG, a basic PERSONALITY dimension of openness and outward-looking sociability that is usually contrasted with INTROVERSION.

extrinsic motivation Doing something for reasons of reward or punishment external to the activity itself. Always contrasted with INTRINSIC MOTIVATION. See FUNCTIONAL AUTONOMY.

eye contact People looking each other in the eye. A form of BEHAVIOUR studied by social scientists as a way of understanding interpersonal distance and relationships in different social situations, both in our own CULTURE, and, comparatively, across cultures.

Eysenck, H. J (born 1916) A leading British exponent of BEHAVIOURIST PSYCHOLOGY noted for his contributions to the theory of PERSONALITY and the construction of personality tests. He has been a controversial figure in the debate about RACE and IQ.

F

fabulation Telling fantastic stories as though they were true – though not involuntarily as in the case of people suffering disturbances of memory (CONFABULATION).

face-to-face group SOCIAL PSYCHOLOGICAL term for a small group of people in close enough physical proximity for each person in the group to interact directly with each of the others. Such a group can usually hold no more than six to eight people.

face validity The extent to which a psychological test or other procedure appears relevant to the VARIABLE it is dealing with.

facework In SOCIAL PSYCHOLOGY, sometimes used to describe social rituals that save 'face' or enhance a public image at the expense of honest EMOTION.

facilitation Making things easier; it is used in reference either to the performance of a given BEHAVIOUR or the transmission of a nerve impulse. See SOCIAL FACILITATION.

factor analysis A statistical technique for analyzing complex CORRELATIONS of scores and tracing the factors underlying these correlations.

faith healing The attempt to heal sickness through a non-rational belief without medical means being used. This belief is usually religious, such as the belief in the healing power of the

Virgin Mary by the people who make a pilgrimage to Lourdes. But people can also have faith in their doctor, even when he has no medicine to help them, or in themselves and their powers of recovery. There is perhaps some ground for believing that faith healing can affect PSYCHOSOMATIC illness; that it can affect organic illness is more dubious.

family therapy Where the family rather than the individual is in PSYCHOTHERAPY, on the assumption that NEUROSIS is the product of disturbed relationships between family members.

fantasy A deliberate act of the imagination in which it is given free rein, usually to experience enjoyable images related to one's WISH-FULFILMENT. Drug-induced fantasy may be very unpleasant however.

father figure Someone who is seen as standing in place of one's real father and who becomes the object of EMOTIONS aroused by the original. More generally an older person, usually in a position of authority, with whom one identifies and looks to for fatherly advice and approval.

fear of failure Like it says. Aroused when a person feels pressured to achieve, and particularly prevalent in people with a high NEED FOR ACHIEVEMENT.

fear of success Mainly used to describe a motive in some women to avoid doing well and achieving success (especially in competition with men) because their SOCIALIZATION has led them to perceive such behaviour as unfeminine.

Fechner's law Large increases in the intensity of a stimulus produce smaller, proportional, increases in the intensity perceived. It is expressed mathematically as $S = k \log R$, where S is the intensity experienced, R is the actual physical intensity and k is a constant. This is one of the first attempts at a mathematical statement of a psychological PHENOMENON. It arose out of the studies in PSYCHOPHYSICS with which PSYCHOLOGY became an experimental science in the 1870s.

feedback A term borrowed from CYBERNETICS where it refers to the direct relationship of the input of a system to its output. The concept of a return flow of output information which can be used to regulate future input is now widely used in PROGRAMMED LEARNING and the development of TEACHING MACHINES.

feeling tone The pleasantness or unpleasantness of the sensation one experiences from the stimulus of a given person, object, or situation.

feminism A social movement or a viewpoint committed to the removal of PREJUDICE against women, differential treatment of men and women, and to the advancement of women's interests in general.

feral child A child supposedly reared by animals in the wild. Such tales are part of the folklore of pop PSYCHOLOGY and should be taken with a large pinch of salt.

fetishism In ANTHROPOLOGY, the worship of a fetish or inanimate object which is believed to possess magic powers. The term has been taken over by CLINICAL PSYCHOLOGY to refer mainly to the sexual excitement in men produced by an object associated with women. Favourite fetishes are hair, feet, shoes, underwear, and black silk stockings.

field In PSYCHOLOGY, this term is sometimes used to denote all the interdependent factors in an organism's environment leading up to a particular piece of BEHAVIOUR.

field independent-dependence The idea that people orient themselves to their environment or FIELD by the use of two distinctly different cognitive styles which are associated with two distinctly different types of PERSONALITY, field independent and field dependent; the former require fewer visual cues from their field and the latter depend on the visual cues from their field for orientation.

field theory In its best known form the GESTALT school of PSYCHOLOGY argued that in the functioning of the BRAIN and in the behaviour of man and the higher animals the whole is greater than the sum of all its parts, that the brain could be understood better as a total FIELD than as a collection of nerve cells, and that the cause of a particular piece of behaviour lies in the totality of a field of interacting elements rather than the most obvious stimulus. In its social applications field theory is closely associated with the work of KURT LEWIN.

field work Any study of human or animal behaviour outside of a laboratory or an EXPERIMENT.

fight-or-flight reaction In zoology, the choices an animal has built into its behavioural repertoire when faced with an intruder to its territory. The term is also used of human BEHAVIOUR in the face of threatened aggression, though it is more often misused to over-simplify behaviour that is far more complex than any animal behaviour.

figural after-effect The perceptual distortion that appears when a second pattern is looked at after a first that is different. The same relationships between FIGURE AND GROUND that were seen in the first pattern tend to be perceived in the second.

figure-and-ground   Apparently one of the psychological prerequisites for PERCEPTION to take place is that the perceptual FIELD is organised as figures distinguished against a relatively homogeneous background. Figure is usually the part of the field that is attended to, though the relationship between figure and ground can switch. The whole phenomenon is best illustrated in an unusual perceptual field like an AMBIGUOUS FIGURE.

fixation   An excessive emotional ATTACHMENT to a person or thing. In PSYCHOANALYSIS, the term implies being stuck in one of the psychosexual stages of CHILDHOOD development (ORAL, ANAL or PHALLIC) and maintaining towards a person or object an ambivalent attachment appropriate to that stage.

fixed-alternative   Test or questionnaire items which require an answer from a given selection of alternatives.

flattening of affect   Weakness or absence of emotional response when a strong response would be appropriate.

flicker fusion frequency   The speed at which a flickering light appears to stop flickering and become continuous. See CRITICAL FLICKER FREQUENCY.

flight into illness   Used in CLINICAL PSYCHOLOGY to describe someone who develops symptoms of illness as a way of escaping conflict. Some social scientists consider this the basis for a great deal of mental illness, especially among poor people living in slums.

floating affect   In PSYCHOANALYSIS, feelings that have become detached from their usual object and are then capable of being attached to another object.

folie à deux   French term meaning 'insanity of two' referring to a DELUSION shared by two people who usually live together.

forced-choice technique   A situation where a subject is forced to choose one of a given series of judgments even though none of them may seem to be appropriate.

forensic psychology   The application of PSYCHOLOGY to the law, usually in regard to criminal behaviour.

forgetting   The loss of the ability to recall something that has been learned. Anything that makes its way into LONG-TERM MEMORY is probably never wholly lost except through BRAIN DAMAGE. Forgetting is likely to be caused by a lack of a stimulus sufficient to retrieve the memory, or else is the result of repressing the memory into the UNCONSCIOUS because of the emotional pain it causes.

formal operations   The fourth, and last, main STAGE in PIAGET's theory of cognitive development, lasting from about 12 to 16 years of age. During this stage the individual becomes able to handle problems involving abstract ideas and to reason logically.

fraternal twins   See DIZYGOTIC TWINS.

free association   One of the techniques used by FREUD in developing PSYCHOANALYSIS. It requires the patient to follow her train of thoughts and images wherever they may lead without any guidance or instructions from the ANALYST. Eventually from the patient's associations the analyst may start to perceive clues about areas of conflict and disturbance that are being surfaced from the UNCONSCIOUS.

free-floating anxiety   A chronic state of irrational ANXIETY that cannot be pinned down to any specific source but can attach itself to anything and everything.

frequency   Either the number of cycles per second of a light or sound wave, or the number of times something occurs in a study.

frequency distribution   A tabulation of the number of times something occurs in a study.

Freud, Sigmund (1856 1939)   Freud's work may be divided into three areas; his invention of PSYCHOANALYSIS as a therapeutic technique, his theory of PERSONALITY, and his social PHILOSOPHY. The origins of Freud's ideas are more overtly personal than those of any other psychologist; it was an attempt to understand himself that led to the development of psychoanalysis. His father's death brought DREAMS that troubled him, and in trying to make sense of them he found the way through to his own UNCONSCIOUS and his unresolved ambivalent feelings about his father – and about the Jewishness his father represented. The result was his first major work, *The Interpretation of Dreams*, widely regarded as his most original and influential book, and the springboard for the rest of his thought.

   On the basis of his own OEDIPUS CONFLICT and of his work with patients, Freud developed a theory of personality which emphasized the crucial importance of the first five years of life in determining the development of the EGO and SUPEREGO and their interrelations with the ID in the adult personality. Freud became increasingly concerned with applying his thinking to the human condition in general and in a series of books, *Totem and*

Taboo, The Future of an Illusion, Civilization and Its Discontents, he worked out the implications of his belief that REPRESSION and its resultant NEUROSIS was the inevitable price mankind paid for civilization.

While each of Freud's ideas is still hotly debated by Freudians and anti-Freudians alike, few people would dispute his enormous and widespread influence in making the 20th century more aware than any previous age of the power of the irrational and the unconscious in human affairs.

Freudian slip A slip of the tongue which FREUD, who denied the existence of randomness or accident in the way a person behaves, interpreted as a clue from the UNCONSCIOUS about a repressed conflict. See also PARAPRAXIS.

frustration-aggression hypothesis The idea that frustration will always lead to aggression in both animals and people, and that aggression always implies some preceding frustration. The exceptions to both postulates are now regarded as perhaps more important than the rule.

F-scale A questionnaire designed during the study of the 'AUTHORITARIAN PERSONALITY' to measure an individual's tendency to authoritarianism (F for fascism). On the basis of individual clinical work and social surveys the designers of the F-scale believed that a potential fascist would score high on the scale, while someone less rigidly conventional, obsessed with power, or subservient to authority, would score low.

fugue From the Latin word for 'flight', a fugue is a relatively long period of AMNESIA in which a person leaves his home, forgets his past, and goes off to start a new and very different life somewhere else. When the UNCONSCIOUS conflict underlying the amnesia has been dealt with the person will remember his old life and IDENTITY and forget the period of the fugue.

functional autonomy The concept, suggested by the American psychologist Gordon Allport, that a particular behaviour which was originally engaged in to achieve a certain goal may itself become a goal. This idea may be relevant in examples of EXTRINSIC MOTIVATION becoming INTRINSIC. For example a child who practises the violin because his parents won't love him or give him any pocket money if he doesn't may come to enjoy the activity of playing the violin for its own sake (and grow up to be a concert musician).

functional disorder Emotional disturbance which cannot be attributed to a physical cause. As a rule of thumb such disturbances are considered NEUROSES and physically-based disorders are considered PSYCHOSES, but this is a gross over-simplification of a very complex problem about which very little is known.

functionalism   A school of PSYCHOLOGY which emphasizes the functions or activities of the MIND rather than its content, which is the emphasis of its rival, STRUCTURALISM.

G

gain-loss theory of interpersonal attraction   An attempt to formulate a theory that takes account of changes in people's liking for each other. It suggests that increases or decreases in the rewarding behaviour we receive from another person have more effect on us than a constant level of liking or disliking. Thus we like best someone who starts out negatively in our estimation and becomes more positive, and we like least a person who starts out positive and becomes negative.

Gallup poll   The first and the best-known technique for the mass sampling of public opinion; invented by the American social scientist George Gallup.

Galton, Francis (1822–1911)   A 19th century British scientist, a cousin and disciple of CHARLES DARWIN, who pioneered the testing of INDIVIDUAL DIFFERENCES in mental abilities.

galvanic skin response   At times of emotional activity, electrical reactions can be detected by electrodes on the surface of the skin. The CORRELATION between the two forms the basis for a LIE DETECTOR test, though like all correlations one is still left guessing as to what it actually means.

game theory   A mathematical approach to the study of conflict and decision-making which treats conflict situations as though they were games, with set tactics and strategies and totally rational players. Some of the simpler situations studied, like the PRISONER'S DILEMMA, have been of interest to SOCIAL PSYCHOLOGISTS looking for MODELS that would generate ideas about social behaviour.

gatekeeping   In SOCIOLOGY, the term for the process by which people are selected in to, or kept out of, the elite circles of a society.

Gaussian curve The BELL-SHAPED CURVE of a NORMAL DISTRIBUTION.

gender identity Belonging, or regarding oneself as belonging, to the male or female sex.

gender role See SEX ROLE.

gene The part of a cell that contains information about HEREDITY.

generalization Making a judgment about a whole category based on experience with a limited part of that category. Ie, a general principle of both science and living.

generalized other According to the American sociologist G H Mead, the concept an individual has of how other people expect him to behave in a given situation. Compare with SIGNIFICANT OTHER.

generation gap Differences between parents and children in ATTITUDES, beliefs, opinions and values, which are attributed at least in part to the effects of being socialized at different times; used to explain conflict between young people and older people. As generation gaps have been evident since the world began there may well be something to this, though the gap may be more apparent then real. See also ZEITGEIST and SOCIALIZATION.

generativity The task of ERIKSON's seventh stage of development to be achieved in middle age. It entails the ability to do creative work or be a creative parent.

genetics The science of HEREDITY.

genital stage In PSYCHOANALYSIS, the mature state of psychosexual development where the individual is capable of a loving, fully sexual relationship. To achieve this stage one must successfully avoid being fixated at one of the earlier stages, ORAL, ANAL or PHALLIC.

genotype An individual's genetically inherited potential. See PHENOTYPE.

gerontology The study of old age and the processes of ageing.

Gesell developmental norms An attempt, by the American psychologist Arnold Gesell, to produce a timetable for the usual appearance of physical abilities in infants and young children.

gestalt A German word meaning a form, a configuration, or a whole, which has properties that are more than just the sum of its parts.

gestalt completion test Incomplete pictures which can only be completed correctly if the subject perceives the underlying unity and wholeness of the picture.

Gestalt psychology A school of PSYCHOLOGY which began in the early part of the 20th century as a reaction against the behavioural psychology of PAVLOV and WATSON, and insisted that psychological phenomena should be treated as GESTALTS which could not be equated with the elements that made them up. The first gestalt psychologists, Kofka, KOHLER, and Wertheimer, arrived at their ideas after studies of PERCEPTION; they were struck by the way the BRAIN organized dots of light into visual patterns, or musical notes into melodies. Kohler later branched out into studies of INSIGHT learning (see the AHA REACTION) in apes, and later gestaltists like Goldstein and LEWIN have extended gestalt ideas into areas of PERSONALITY and SOCIAL PSYCHOLOGY. Gestalt thinking on perception is now largely accepted by psychologists, though many people would argue that there are areas of human BEHAVIOUR which can still best be understood by an analysis of the elements involved.

gestures Bodily movements for the purpose of communication.

glossolalia 'Speaking in tongues'; babbling in what sounds like an unknown language (but isn't). Associated mainly with religious ecstasy but also found in people who are emotionally very disturbed.

goal-directed behaviour Animal BEHAVIOUR that can only be understood by assuming that it is intended to achieve a particular goal.

Goodenough test An INTELLIGENCE TEST for children, invented by Florence Goodenough, where the subject is asked to draw a picture of a man.

gradient A regular rate of change between two conditions or VARIABLES.

grand mal See EPILEPSY.

graphology The use of handwriting as a kind of PROJECTIVE TECHNIQUE, where a person's handwriting is analyzed for whatever it may reveal about his PERSONALITY.

grasping reflex The automatic response by fingers or toes when the palm or the sole of the foot is stimulated.

great-man theory The idea that the course of events is influenced at crucial times by the actions of outstanding men. As a way of understanding history it is a gross over-simplification.

group dynamics The study of the way people behave in groups, especially small or FACE-TO-FACE GROUPS. Associated with the pioneering work of KURT LEWIN.

grouping   The statistical process of combining individual scores into categories or ranking them as, for example, PERCENTILES.

group mind   A hypothetical entity, sometimes given mystical qualities, which has been suggested as the agency for crowds acting in unison. It is a way of saying we don't understand very much about CROWD BEHAVIOUR.

group norm   Behaviour expected of all the members of a group. See NORM.

group test   A PAPER-AND-PENCIL test given simultaneously to a large group of people.

group therapy   PSYCHOTHERAPY involving several people at the same time. The assumption is that people can benefit from the experiences and companionship of other people.

groupthink   George Orwell's term for the totalitarian imposition of authorized thoughts on all the members of a society. Taken over by some SOCIAL PSYCHOLOGISTS interested in the way that members of very cohesive groups can become so preoccupied with maintaining a group consensus of thought that their critical faculties become dulled.

GSR   Galvanic skin response. Known in North America as PSYCHOGALVANIC REFLEX.

guiding fiction   A concept, proposed by ALFRED ADLER, that people have constant principles by which they evaluate their experiences and behaviour. These guiding fictions form the background to people's lives and often unconsciously influence the basic elements of their character.

guilt   The AWARENESS of having violated a SOCIAL NORM of behaviour one identifies with, and feeling regret as a result. In PSYCHO-ANALYSIS guilt is the result of UNCONSCIOUS conflict where the SUPEREGO predominates and produces symptoms of NEUROSIS if the conflict is unresolved.

guilt culture   A CULTURE which relies on its members' consciences and feelings of GUILT to maintain order and social control. Such a culture is vulnerable to the ANTISOCIAL PERSONALITY, a person incapable of feeling guilt. Contrasted with a SHAME CULTURE.

H

habit   A learned response to a given situation which occurs in such a regular fashion that it appears to be virtually automatic – so it may even be mistaken for INNATE behaviour and considered an INSTINCT.

habituation   In EXPERIMENTAL PSYCHOLOGY, decreasing response to a stimulus as it becomes more familiar through repeated presentation. With reference to drug use habituation is the condition, resulting from repeated use of a drug, where there is a psychological, though not a physical, DEPENDENCE on the drug but with little or no desire to increase the dose.

hallucination   A perceptual ILLUSION of a vivid experience that has no apparent reality in the external world. Usually associated with PSYCHOSIS, though it can happen to anyone. Can also be drug-induced by the use of HALLUCINOGENS or PSYCHEDELIC drugs.

hallucinogen   A drug, like LSD or mescaline, that induces HALLUCINATIONS.

halo effect   In SOCIAL PSYCHOLOGY, the tendency to GENERALIZE, in judging a person, from one characteristic (usually positive) to a total impression.

Hawthorne effect   Paying attention to people at work improves their performance. The findings of a study done at the Hawthorne works of the Western Electric Company in California. Various attempts by the management to improve workers' conditions were made; they included changes in lighting, rest breaks, hours of work, and systems of payment. Each of these changes resulted in an increase in productivity – and so did a return to the original conditions of work. The investigators concluded that the changes in the external environment had not influenced the workers' performance so much as their PERCEPTION that people were interested in them and their work. An example of SOCIAL FACILITATION.

hearing loss   The degeneration of an individual's hearing ability. Apart from physical damage or disease it is caused by prolonged exposure to noise (figure 13).

hebephrenia   One of the common forms of psychological disturbance classified as SCHIZOPHRENIA. It is characterized by giggling and silliness and displays of inappropriate EMOTIONS.

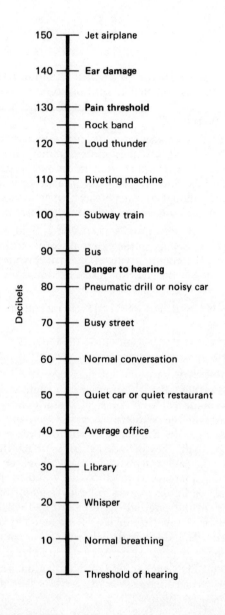

Figure 13 Hearing loss and the loudness of some familiar sounds

60

hedonic   Relating to pleasure or the dimension of pleasure versus pain.

hedonism   In PSYCHOLOGY, the idea that all of our behaviour is motivated by a need to pursue pleasure and avoid pain; in PHILOSOPHY, the doctrine that it is our ethical duty to do so. The one does not imply the other.

helplessness, learned   See LEARNED HELPLESSNESS.

heredity   The biological transmission of characteristics from parents to offspring.·

heritage   Everything transmitted from one generation to another, whether individually by HEREDITY or socially by custom, language, religion and tradition, and physical possessions.

hermaphrodite   A person or animal with both male and female sex organs.

heterosexuality   Being attracted by the opposite sex; the NORM in most societies and generally considered to be psychologically NORMAL as well, though the implication that any other kind of sexuality is therefore ABNORMAL is now thought to be a dubious or over-simplified proposition.

heuristic   An idea or method of teaching that stimulates further thinking and discovery.

hidden-figure   See EMBEDDED FIGURE.

higher mental processes   Thinking (including learning, memory and imagination) as opposed to sensing.

higher-order conditioning   A technique used in CLASSICAL CONDITIONING in which a previously established CONDITIONED STIMULUS serves as the UNCONDITIONED STIMULUS for a new EXPERIMENT.

holistic   Relating to the basic tenet of GESTALT PSYCHOLOGY that behaviour cannot be explained by reducing it to its simplest units.

holophrastic speech   A form of speech where single words are used to convey complex meaning. Found in primitive languages and in the earliest speech of all children.

homeostasis   Physiological term for the maintenance of balance or equilibrium within a complex system like the human body or its sub-systems like temperature and oxygen level. See SERVOMECHANISM.

homologous   Anatomical term for organs with similar origins in different species (like a human arm and a fish's fin), but which may have different functions.

homophobia Literally, a PHOBIA about men; used of apparently HETEROSEXUAL men who are threatened by overt male HOMOSEXUALITY.

homosexuality Being attracted by people of the same sex. Contrast with HETEROSEXUALITY. See also LESBIANISM.

horizontal-vertical illusion An optical ILLUSION in which a vertical line appears to be longer than a horizontal line of equal length.

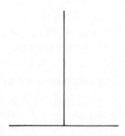

Figure 14 Horizontal–vertical illusion

horopter When both eyes are fixated on the same point, the horopter is the locus of all the points in the external world whose images stimulate corresponding points on both RETINAE and are thus perceived as single images.

human engineering See ERGONOMICS.

humanistic psychology A school of PSYCHOLOGY which emphasizes the qualities that differentiate human beings from other animals, particularly creativity, humour, play, and psychological growth in general. Sometimes called the 'THIRD FORCE' as opposed to BEHAVIOURISM and PSYCHOANALYSIS. Its leading proponents are Gordon Allport, ABRAHAM MASLOW and CARL ROGERS.

human performance factors An American term for ERGONOMICS.

Huntington's chorea An inherited progressively degenerative disease of the nervous system.

hydrocephalus Excessive amount of cerebrospinal fluid within the skull, resulting in an enlarged skull and underdeveloped BRAIN.

hydrophobia Medical term for a symptom in man of the disease rabies meaning literally 'fear of water'. The fear in this case is not psychologically ABNORMAL but a symptom of the disease.

hyperthyroidism   Excessive secretions by the thyroid gland that seem to cause heightened activity and excitement.

hypnosis   An induced condition of extreme suggestibility to the hypnotist. The typical hypnotic trance looks like sleep but is probably a very different state – the EEGs of people in hypnosis are apparently different from patterns associated with sleep. Despite the long history of interest in hypnosis not much is understood about the condition. But it is clearly a real and potentially powerful PHENOMENON. As far back as the mid-19th century two British surgeons, Braid and Esdaile, were performing successful battlefield surgery using hypnosis as a general anaesthetic. This development stopped with the invention of chloroform.

hypnotherapy   The use of HYPNOSIS in PSYCHOTHERAPY.

hypochondria   NEUROTIC concern for one's health.

hypothalamus   A region at the base of the BRAIN concerned with the regulation of bodily processes.

hypothesis   An explanation for observed data which still has to be tested.

hypothetico-deductive method   The accepted method of conducting scientific investigations, first formulated by Galileo in the 17th century, in which a scientist observes something he doesn't understand, comes up with a tentative explanation or HYPOTHESIS from which he can deduce a testable outcome, and sees whether his predicted outcome is verified by observation.

hysteria   From the Greek word for 'womb' because it was thought that the emotional disturbances it described were exclusively female and caused by disorders of the womb. There is no general agreement on the symptoms of hysteria, though most authorities seem to regard DISSOCIATION as one defining characteristic. There are several recognized forms of hysteria, the most striking being CONVERSION HYSTERIA. PSYCHOANALYSIS regards all hysteria as NEUROSIS, the product of UNCONSCIOUS conflict.

hysterical paralysis   See CONVERSION HYSTERIA.

I

iconic memory   The image of a visual stimulus that lasts for a second or two.

id From the Latin word for 'it'; according to FREUD, the id houses the deepest UNCONSCIOUS drives which are most in touch with the biological nature of the body and is one of the three main aspects of the PERSONALITY. The id is dominated by the PLEASURE PRINCIPLE, and causes problems for the EGO when its DRIVES are blocked.

ideal self Holding certain values and standards for oneself (one's SELF) and striving to realise them.

idée fixe French for 'fixed idea'; a persistent OBSESSION that is impervious to contradictory evidence or argument.

identical twins See MONOZYGOTIC TWINS.

identification In general terms, recognizing the IDENTITY or nature of someone or something; in PSYCHOANALYSIS, emulating the behaviour of a person with whom one has a powerful emotional bond.

identity Having essentially unchanging characteristics; the basic unity of a PERSONALITY, especially the SELF-IMAGE.

identity formation The task of ERIKSON's fifth stage of PERSONALITY development, in ADOLESCENCE, where the individual has to find his own personal IDENTITY.

idiot savant French for 'scholarly idiot'; a person who appears to be mentally retarded but possesses outstanding mental abilities in one area. Idiots savants are part of the folklore of pop PSYCHOLOGY and are rarely encountered today. The contradiction they represent is probably more apparent than real; if there is anything to their abilities it is doubtful if they are really mentally retarded, and if they are really mentally retarded their abilities may be no more than tricks of memory.

illusion A mistake in PERCEPTION either for physical reasons (an optical illusion like an IMPOSSIBLE FIGURE) or psychological reasons as in HALLUCINATION.

imageless thought A thought or sequence of thoughts with no accompanying image or sensation. Whether such thoughts exist has been debated since the time of the ancient Greeks; the weight of modern opinion among psychologists is that they do.

imago In PSYCHOANALYTIC thought, an idealized representation of a person, usually a parent, which was formed in the UNCONSCIOUS during early CHILDHOOD. The imago remains the same into adulthood where it can have a powerful influence on BEHAVIOUR, especially in providing MODELS for that person to fall in love with and become emotionally involved with in general.

imitation Copying another person's BEHAVIOUR whether as a CONSCIOUS or an UNCONSCIOUS act. See also MODELLING

immanent justice The idea that punishment for wrong doing is absolute and inevitable; that even if undetected, wrong doing will be followed by retribution in the form of accidents or bad luck imposed on the miscreant by a higher power, like God. According to PIAGET such thinking is typical of EGOCENTRIC children below the age of eight (or perhaps eighty).

immunization See INOCULATION.

implicit personality theory Generally, the unquestioned assumptions an individual uses in thinking about the PERSONALITY of another person; specifically, the characteristics that tend to be associated with each other in judging someone's personality. For example, 'warm' usually goes with 'outgoing', 'sociable', and 'good-humoured'; 'cold' with 'withdrawn', 'reserved', and 'humourless'. The concept is particularly associated with the American SOCIAL PSYCHOLOGIST Fritz Heider.

impossible figure A drawing of a figure which can only be perceived as contradictory.

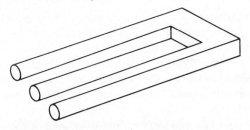

Figure 15 Impossible figure of a tuning fork
(from *Principles of General Psychology*, 4th edition, G A Kimble, N Ganvegy and E Zigler, New York, Ronald Press, 1974, p 371)

impression management Associated with the Canadian sociologist Erving Goffman; the attempt to present oneself (one's SELF) to other people in such a way that they will react in a controllable or predictable fashion.

imprinting In ETHOLOGY, a form of learning in very young animals at certain CRITICAL PERIODS. The learning is rapid and usually irreversible. For instance, some species of baby ducks will follow the first moving object they encounter after being hatched. This object, on which they are imprinted, is usually their mother, but, as KONRAD LORENZ showed, it could just as easily be an ethologist. Imprinting is thus a useful biological mechanism, in an inflexible and limited kind of way, which includes most of the behaviour usually termed as INSTINCTIVE.

inappropriate affect An emotional response that is grossly out of touch with the needs of the situation, eg laughing at a tragic event. Often regarded as a symptom of PSYCHOSIS.

incest Sexual intercourse between close relatives; how close and how related will vary from CULTURE to culture, but apparently the TABOO against it is universal.

incidental learning Learning that takes place without a CONSCIOUS effort, eg, learning the names of shops on the way to the bus stop.

incremental learning Learning that takes place in a series of regular and orderly steps rather than following flashes of INSIGHT.

independent variable The VARIABLE in a study whose changes are the basis for predictions, because they are not DEPENDENT upon changes in any other variable in the study. The most familiar example of an independent variable is an EXPERIMENTAL VARIABLE.

individual differences The comparison of people's characteristics and performance, especially INTELLIGENCE and INTELLIGENCE TEST scores.

industrial psychology The branch of PSYCHOLOGY that deals with the world of work including selection, training, job satisfaction, the environment, human relationships on the job, and ERGONOMICS.

infantile amnesia FORGETTING the memories of earliest CHILDHOOD explained by PSYCHOANALYSIS as REPRESSION. The non-existence of language with which to 'fix' experience in the memory is also suggested as a cause.

infantile birth theories A young child's answer to the question 'where do babies come from?' The navel appears to be a firm favourite.

infantile sexuality The concept that made FREUD a pariah to the Viennese medical establishment; the idea that infants can have sexual experiences, that the capacity to feel pleasure when the EROGENOUS ZONES are stimulated is present from birth.

infantilism The condition of someone who has not developed psychologically beyond infancy, or who represses to that state when older.

inferential statistics Procedures by which GENERALIZATIONS can be made from findings on representative samples to the larger groups from which they are drawn.

inferiority complex According to ALFRED ADLER, an UNCONSCIOUS condition where the individual feels inadequate and resentful, often because of some physical feature regarded as a defect. This complex leads to distorted behaviours, the most striking of which is OVERCOMPENSATION for the perceived defect – a mechanism often invoked to explain aggressiveness in small men.

information theory A study of the nature of information and the way it is communicated. It was originated by mathematicians and engineers and draws heavily on concepts from these fields, but with advances in BRAIN research it has been used by psychologists and linguists.

inhibition The blocking of one physiological or psychological process by another, eg, the response to one sense receptor inhibiting response to another, or fear inhibiting escape from danger. In PSYCHOANALYSIS inhibition is used to describe an impulse from the ID being blocked from entering CONSCIOUSNESS by the SUPEREGO. This is not the same as REPRESSION where the impulse is actively held back.

inkblot test See RORSCHACH TEST.

innate A tendency that is present at birth though it may not become active until later life.

innate releasing mechanism A concept introduced by Nikolaas Tinbergen, a European pioneer of ETHOLOGY. His observations of stickleback fish led him to wonder how male sticklebacks, who never saw a female until they were sexually mature, knew to chase away certain sticklebacks (ie, males) and to woo others (ie, females). The fish were reacting to the presence of red colouring on the male's belly or its absence on the female's. This was the mechanism that released their INNATE response.

inner-directed A term introduced to SOCIOLOGY in the United States by David Riesman to describe people who react to pressures of social change on the basis of personal values internalized early in life. Contrast with OUTER-DIRECTED and TRADITION-DIRECTED.

inoculation In SOCIAL PSYCHOLOGY, a technique for strengthening a person's ATTITUDE and his resistance to persuasion by exposing him to a small dose of the opposing attitude.

insight learning The appearance of understanding, usually sudden, in dealing with a problem. Insight involves both the finding of a cognitive solution to a practical problem (as in the AHA REACTION) and the self-knowledge that can be achieved in PSYCH-OTHERAPY. Contrast with TRIAL AND ERROR LEARNING.

instinct An INNATE unlearned tendency or impulse which is fixed and unchanging and shared by all the members of a species. When a particular form of BEHAVIOUR is termed instinctive in an animal it becomes the province of ETHOLOGY. Referring to any form of human behaviour as instinctive leads immediately to heated controversy bedevilled by politics and ideology. In any event the concept appears to be of dubious value in understanding any particular piece of human behaviour, most of which is learned.

institutional racism Racially PREJUDICED behaviour that has not been adopted CONSCIOUSLY but is simply the consequence of conforming to the NORMS and conventions of a society whose institutions of law, government, and business systematically discriminate against particular racial groups.

instrumental aggression A term sometimes used in SOCIAL PSYCHOLOGY to describe behaviour that is not aggressive for its own sake but as a means to an end. For example, the difference between killing an enemy in person and pressing a button in a missile site a thousand miles away.

instrumental conditioning See OPERANT CONDITIONING.

integration The process of organizing different parts into a whole of a higher order; used widely in science, from the organization of nervous impulses necessary for any kind of behaviour, to the organization of a whole society.

intellectualizing Dealing with a situation solely in intellectual terms and ignoring or denying the EMOTION involved. In PSYCHO-ANALYSIS, it is regarded as a form of DEFENCE MECHANISM to protect the EGO from unpleasant feelings.

intelligence Although psychologists have been discussing this concept since the 1870s there is no general agreement on what intelligence is. Most psychologists would probably agree that HEREDITY sets the limits of a person's intelligence, and most would agree that the ability to learn in one form or another (handling abstract ideas, adapting to new situations, perceiving complex relationships) is a sign of high intelligence – which doesn't get us very far but has never prevented psychologists from designing new INTELLIGENCE TESTS. Intelligence is a good example of a PHENOTYPE.

intelligence quotient A score obtained from an INTELLIGENCE TEST by dividing the MENTAL AGE obtained on the test by the actual or chronological age and multiplying by 100, ie, IQ = $^{MA}/_{CA}$ x 100. An IQ score by itself is meaningless; it does not measure intelligence the way a tape measures height, for instance. It is only a measure of comparison between all the people who have taken that particular test, with the average score being placed arbitrarily at around 100.

intelligence test A test that is supposed to measure INTELLIGENCE whatever that may be. Its purpose is to discriminate between people who score high and people who score low (ie, high and low IQ), for the purpose of assigning them to various educational, occupational, and social categories. High scores are supposed to denote high intelligence, and vice versa, but in the absence of an agreed definition of intelligence the OPERATIONAL DEFINITION becomes circular – people score high on intelligence tests because they are highly intelligent because highly intelligent people score high on intelligence tests. There is also a great deal of evidence that intelligence tests tend to be biased in favour of white, urban, middle-class people in their selection of test items. See also BINET.

interaction process analysis A technique for recording and analyzing the interactions between people in a FACE-TO-FACE GROUP.

interaction recorder A device for timing different kinds of interaction in FACE-TO-FACE GROUPS.

intercorrelations A table of CORRELATIONS between each and every one of a series of VARIABLES.

interference Two principal meanings in PSYCHOLOGY; the change in PERCEPTION when two light or sound waves out of phase come together, and more commonly where one kind of learning INHIBITS or disturbs another.

intermittent reinforcement In a CONDITIONING EXPERIMENT only intermittently rewarding an animal for making correct responses rather than continuously. This appears to produce slower but more strongly established conditioning.

internalization Accepting external ideas or values as one's own to the point of not being aware of their origins. The best known example of this concept is the SUPEREGO, where the values of the parents and the parent society are internalized into the developing PERSONALITY.

internal justification In SOCIAL PSYCHOLOGY, a way of resolving COGNITIVE DISSONANCE which underlies the most powerful kind of ATTITUDE change. Eg if you feel, on reflection, that you have an awful job you can resolve (psychologically) the dissonance between the COGNITIONS 'I am a sensible person' and 'I choose to work in an awful job' either externally or internally. An external justification might be 'I do it for the money', but that wouldn't change your opinion of the job. However if you began to consider the job in a different light and saw its more positive aspects you would be justifying your decision to work in an awful job internally. You would in fact be persuading yourself, the most powerful way of changing someone's attitudes.

interpersonal attraction General term for an area of SOCIAL PSYCHOLOGY concerned with why people are attracted to each other. See GAIN-LOSS THEORY OF INTERPERSONAL ATTRACTION.

interposition A situation where one object is partially obscuring another to provide a background cue in the PERCEPTION of distance.

intervening variable An inferred process of a hypothetical VARIABLE that is supposed to occur between a stimulus and a response. See BLACK BOX.

interviewer bias The effects on an interview of the CONSCIOUS or UNCONSCIOUS biases (assumptions, expectations) of the interviewer. Sometimes extended to include the whole process from constructing the interview schedule to interpreting the data. See also EXPERIMENTER BIAS, ROSENTHAL EFFECT and SELF-FULFILLING PROPHECY.

intrapsychic Refers to conflicts or processes that take place within the PSYCHE (ie the MIND, PERSONALITY or SELF).

intrinsic motivation Doing something for its own sake, because the activity itself is rewarding. Always contrasted with EXTRINSIC MOTIVATION. See FUNCTIONAL AUTONOMY.

intropunitive Blaming and punishing oneself, or feeling guilty and humiliated, in response to frustration. Contrast with EXTRAPUNITIVE.

introspection The process of examining and reporting on the contents of one's own MIND.

introversion According to JUNG, a basic PERSONALITY dimension of being withdrawn, inward looking, and passive, that is usually contrasted with EXTRAVERSION.

invert Little used clinical term for a male HOMOSEXUAL.

involution   Literally the opposite of EVOLUTION, ie decline or deterioration; used of mid-life physical and psychological crises and changes. See INVOLUTIONAL MELANCHOLIA and MIDDLESCENCE.

involutional melancholia   A state of DEPRESSION and ANXIETY associated traditionally with menopause and with mid-life crises in general.

IQ   See INTELLIGENCE QUOTIENT.

IRM   See INNATE RELEASING MECHANISM.

irrational   Something that is inconsistent with logic or reason.

Ishihara test   A test for COLOUR BLINDNESS in which the subject has to pick out a pattern against a complex background of different colours. People with normal COLOUR VISION can perceive the pattern and colour blind people cannot.

isomorphic   An old idea, re-introduced by GESTALT PSYCHOLOGY, that there is a one-to-one correspondence between a perceived stimulus and its representation in the BRAIN. The concept has now largely been abandoned.

item analysis   A technique to determine the effectiveness of different items on a test for discriminating between the people who take it.

J

James-Lange theory of emotions   A fusion of two similar theories of the EMOTIONS put forward by the American philosopher William James and the Danish physiologist C G Lange. In essence they suggest that what we refer to as emotion is our CONSCIOUS AWARENESS of the bodily changes that follow an exciting event. Thus it would be more correct to say that we are sad because we cry, rather than that we cry because we are sad. Contrast with BARD-CANNON THEORY.

J curve   A FREQUENCY DISTRIBUTION of conforming behaviour portraying on a graph that the behaviour of most people will fall at or near the behaviour expected. For example, in Western countries if a dinner party is at eight most people will arrive at 8.0 o'clock give or take a few minutes, with one or two people (usually the ones who stopped to ask for directions) arriving very late. The shape of the curve is actually a reverse capital J.

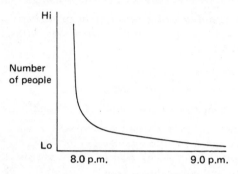

Figure 16 J curve

jnd See JUST NOTICEABLE DIFFERENCE.

job analysis One of the key ROLES of INDUSTRIAL PSYCHOLOGISTS where the elements of a job are studied in an attempt to match the tasks to be performed with the workers' abilities to perform them.

Jones, Ernest (1879–1958) A British PYSCHOANALYST who was one of FREUD's earliest followers and later wrote the official biography of Freud.

Jung, Carl Gustav (1875–1961) Jung was a Swiss PSYCHOAN-ALYST, one of FREUD's earliest colleagues. For about six years they were very close and Freud regarded Jung as the heir apparent to the movement he had founded. Jung was a PSYCHIATRIST of some status and, importantly for Freud, he was a Christian, the son of a Protestant minister. Jung left the Freudian movement in 1914 and founded his own, largely because he could not accept Freud's uncompromising stand on the fundamental importance of sex in the origin of NEUROSIS. Jung's interests were also more mystically inclined than Freud's devotion to rationality could tolerate – Jung studied practically everything from alchemy to yoga. See especially ARCHETYPES, COLLECTIVE UNCONSCIOUS and INTROVERSION–EXTRAVERSION.

just noticeable difference The minimum amount of difference that a subject can detect between two stimuli.

just-world hypothesis In SOCIAL PSYCHOLOGY, the term used for the unquestioned assumption that the world is a just place, where the deserving are rewarded and the undeserving punished.

It therefore follows that if people are punished they must have done something to deserve it, and this is how the HYPOTHESIS accounts for people who blame victims for their own misfortunes. See also DISTRIBUTIVE JUSTICE.

K

Kent-Rosanoff test   A FREE ASSOCIATION test of 100 words together with a standardized list of the relative FREQUENCY of people's responses to them.

kinaesthetic   Refers to the sense that deals with movement of the body and the limbs. See PROPRIOCEPTORS.

Kinsey report   The first large-scale survey of human sexual behaviour, carried out in the United States in the 1940s and 1950s. Still regarded as an illuminating pioneer work despite the inevitable heavy criticism of its methodology.

kinship system   In ANTHROPOLOGY the web of family relationships and the behaviour associated with them.

Klein, Melanie (1882–1960)   A pioneer in the PSYCHOANALYSIS of children and of research into DEPRESSION. Kleinians still consider themselves Freudian while differing on several major points of theory.

kleptomania   A COMPULSION to steal. See also MANIA.

Kohler, Wolfgang (1887–1967)   One of the founders of GESTALT PSYCHOLOGY. His primary contribution was his work on INSIGHT LEARNING with apes, during which he discovered the AHA REACTION.

Korsakoff's syndrome   A memory disorder, due mostly to alcoholism.

Kraepelin, Emil (1856–1926)   A German PSYCHIATRIST who suggested a classification for PSYCHOSES that is still the basis of present usage.

Krafft-Ebing, Richard von (1840–1903)   A German PSYCHIATRIST who pioneered the scientific study of human sexual behaviour and took the most detailed interest in sexual perversions.

Kuder Preference Record A questionnaire designed to elicit a subject's areas of vocational interest.

L

labelling theory In SOCIAL PSYCHOLOGY, this is a way of explaining deviant behaviour by focusing on the reactions of other people to the person they label deviant. When combined with SELF-FULFILLING PROPHECY labelling theory has also been used to account for psychotic behaviour. Thus if a person is labelled PARANOID everything she does is interpreted in the light of her paranoia and invariably taken as evidence for the correctness of the original diagnosis.

labile The free and swiftly changing expression of EMOTION.

Laing, Ronald D (born 1927) A Scottish PSYCHIATRIST whose comprehensive criticism of traditional psychiatric diagnosis and treatment have been fairly influential. A leading figure in the EXISTENTIAL PSYCHIATRY movement, Laing is particularly concerned with the origins of emotional disturbance within the system of family relationships.

Lamarckianism A theory of EVOLUTION proposed by the 19th century French biologist Henri Lamarck and suggesting that an animal's ACQUIRED CHARACTERISTICS could be genetically transmitted to its offspring. Scientists have generally preferred DARWIN's rival theory of evolution.

latency period In PSYCHOANALYSIS, the period between age four or five and the beginning of ADOLESCENCE when interest in sex is either non-existent or SUBLIMATED.

latent content In PSYCHOANALYSIS, the hidden REPRESSED meaning of a dream. Compare with MANIFEST CONTENT.

latent learning See INCIDENTAL LEARNING.

laterality Literally 'sidedness'; preferring either the left hand or foot, for instance, for a task that can be accomplished with either. See BILATERAL TRANSFER.

lateral thinking A term suggested by Edward De Bono to describe an attempt to solve a problem by other than the usual methods, thus allowing the problem to be re-conceptualized and perhaps solved by a previously unacceptable or unthought of solution.

law of parsimony   See OCCAM's RAZOR.

laws of association   The principle underlying the connections in the memory between certain ideas, feelings, or behaviours. Aristotle made the first formulation of these principles in the fourth century BC.

lay analyst   The name given to a PSYCHOANALYST without a medical degree.

learned helplessness   The idea that animals and people who have previously been in a situation where they could not avoid being punished learn that they are helpless, and continue to react passively to being punished even when they do in fact have the power to avoid the punishment.

learning curve   The curve obtained by plotting on a graph measured changes in learning performance over time.

learning plateau   A flattening of the LEARNING CURVE due to a temporary halt in learning progress.

learning set   Sometimes described as 'learning how to learn'; a generalized approach to problems in which animals or people carry over to a new learning situation the responses and strategies they learned in a previous situation. TRANSFER OF TRAINING results from a learning set.

learning theory   An attempt to explain the process of learning.

lesbianism   Female HOMOSEXUALITY; the word 'homosexual' can be applied to women because it is derived from the Greek 'homos' (same) rather than the Latin 'homo' (man). Lesbian is derived from the Greek island of Lesbos, which in antiquity was associated with female homosexuality.

lesion   Damage to bodily tissue from accident, disease or surgery. In the study of behaviour the term usually refers to BRAIN lesions.

level of aspiration   The goals or standards of performance a person sets for himself.

levels of significance   See STATISTICAL SIGNIFICANCE.

Lewin, Kurt (1890–1947)   A student of the early GESTALT PSYCHOLOGISTS who applied some of their thinking to SOCIAL PSYCHOLOGY where he pioneered the field of GROUP DYNAMICS.

libido   FREUD's term for sexual energy, the driving force of human behaviour. In his later writings he used the term more diffusely to cover all kinds of psychic energy. Generally speaking the term is currently used to denote energy whose origins at least are sexual and which is dynamic and irrational in expression.

lie detector An instrument for monitoring physiological changes like heart rate and electrical resistance of the skin under conditions of emotional STRESS. The assumption is that the subject will show signs of emotional upheaval if he lies in answer to a question. It's a big assumption.

life space A term introduced by LEWIN to describe the totality of the physical and psychological factors in the environment of an individual or group at any one time.

Likert scale A technique, developed by the American social scientist Rensis Likert, for constructing ATTITUDE measures where the subject indicates on a three or five point scale whether he agrees or disagrees with a particular statement.

limbic system A group of BRAIN structures thought to be particularly important in the regulation of EMOTION and MOTIVATION. Part of the area sometimes known as the OLD BRAIN.

limen See THRESHOLD.

linguistic determinism The HYPOTHESIS that the possible thoughts available to people are shaped by their language.

linguistic relativity See LINGUISTIC DETERMINISM.

Little Albert The child conditioned by J B WATSON to fear rats.

Little Hans A young patient whom FREUD cured of a PHOBIA about horses.

Lloyd Morgan's Canon The principle, suggested by the comparative psychologist Lloyd Morgan in 1894, that any interpretation of an animal's BEHAVIOUR must be the simplest possible to account for what is observed. Thus an explanation requiring a higher psychological functioning should not be offered if a lower will suffice. A special case of OCCAM'S RAZOR.

lobotomy The commonest form of PSYCHOSURGERY, where the frontal lobes are severed from the main part of the BRAIN. Formerly used as a last resort for severe DEPRESSION but much less common now.

localization In general, placing the source of a particular stimulus; the most common usage is perhaps in NEUROPHYSIOLOGY where localization refers to the attempt to attribute particular functions to particular areas of the BRAIN. See also BRAIN LOCALIZATION.

locus of control A PERSONALITY dimension in which people who have an internal locus feel they have control over what happens to them, and people with an external locus tend to attribute their experiences to outside forces or other people.

long-term memory Permanent, as opposed to SHORT-TERM MEMORY or to SENSORY MEMORY.

looking-glass self In SOCIOLOGY, the part of a person's SELF-IMAGE that is based on the reactions or judgments of other people; suggested by the American sociologists C H Cooley and G H Mead.

Lorenz, Konrad (born 1903) A pioneer of ETHOLOGY whose books *King Solomon's Ring* and *On Aggression* helped popularize the subject.

Lowenfeld test A PROJECTIVE TECHNIQUE in which the subject is asked to make anything he likes out of hundreds of little pieces of wood in different shapes, sizes and colours.

M

MA See MENTAL AGE.

Machiavellianism A PERSONALITY characteristic in which a person manipulates others for his own gain,

magic thinking Any attempt to understand and manipulate the human condition by recourse to supernatural powers. In particular the term is used to describe the belief that there is a causal link between one's wishes and the real world, that 'wishing can make it so'. Said to be typical of children, psychotics, and primitive peoples. Would that I had a tenner for every 'normal' adult in our own advanced civilization who engages in magic thinking.

mandala In JUNG's theories, a magic circle that represents the striving for total unity of the SELF. The idea comes from symbols of the cosmos found in different CULTURES.

mania Uncontrollable excitement accompanied by the impulse to perform a particular kind of BEHAVIOUR.

manic BEHAVIOUR characterized by a MANIA.

manic-depressive A PSYCHOSIS typified by extreme swings of mood from the wild excitement of MANIA to the inadequacy and ANXIETY of deep DEPRESSION. In 'normal' people the swings range from 'being high' to 'having the blues'.

manifest content In PSYCHOANALYSIS, the CONSCIOUS expression of the REPRESSED LATENT CONTENT; the surface account of a DREAM that is most easily remembered and reported.

Manikin test A crude test of gross mental ability where the subject has to reassemble the parts of a small wooden figure of a man.

mantra A word or phrase repeated over and over as an aid to meditation.

marasmus Severe physiological weakness found in infants suffering from a DEPRIVATION of either food or love.

marginality In SOCIAL SCIENCE, a term used to denote the effects on an individual or group of being excluded from the mainstream of a society.

masking The blocking of one sensory stimulus or process by another.

Maslow, Abraham (1908–1970) An American personality theorist and leading exponent of HUMANISTIC PSYCHOLOGY; closely associated with the terms PEAK EXPERIENCE and SELF-ACTUALIZATION.

masochism The experience of sexual pleasure through suffering physical pain. Usually considered a sexual perversion. Named after Sader Masoch, an exponent of the subject. In PSYCHOANALYSIS, masochism is seen as a form of turning one's destructive DRIVES inwards. Usually coupled with SADISM as SADO-MASOCHISM.

massed practice A technique of learning in which the lessons or periods of practice follow each other without a break. A much less effective method of learning than DISTRIBUTED PRACTICE, with which it is usually contrasted.

masturbation Stimulation of one's own sex organs.

maternal deprivation The lack of care and love provided by a mother or mothering figure. Especially important during the first three years of life, the optimum period for the forming of social ATTACHMENTS. Maternal deprivation, in children who have been institutionalized or abandoned, frequently leads to physical, psychological, or social problems in later life. See BOWLBY.

matriarchy A society or a social group run by women. Contrast with PATRIARCHY.

matrilineal A society or social group where descent or inheritance is traced through the female line. Contrast with PATRILINEAL.

maturation In PSYCHOLOGY, the processes of growth and development which are common to all the members of a species and appear regardless of individual HEREDITY or environment. It is a concept that cuts right across the NATURE-NURTURE PROBLEM.

maze A device for studying learning in both animals and humans, ranging from a single T-junction with a choice of two pathways to an extremely complex labyrinth.

McNaughten rules A mid 19th century legal ruling that is still widely used in deciding whether a criminal defendant is insane and therefore not responsible for his actions. The ruling states that a person is criminally liable unless his reason was so defective that he did not realize the nature of his action, or that it was wrong.

Mead, Margaret (1901–1979) An American ANTHROPOLOGIST whose work on CHILDHOOD and ADOLESCENCE in the South Pacific included some pioneering cross-cultural work on sexual and SEX-ROLE behaviour.

mean In STATISTICS the most commonly used MEASURE OF CENTRAL TENDENCY. It is the arithmetic average, found by summing the values of a group of numbers and dividing by the total.

measures of central tendency The three STATISTICS which can each be used as a central value to describe a group of numbers, the MEAN, the MEDIAN, and the MODE.

median In STATISTICS, it is the MEASURE OF CENTRAL TENDENCY which divides a group of scores in half, with half the scores falling above the median score and half below.

mediate Sometimes used in PSYCHOLOGY to describe an activity, often cognitive, that comes between a stimulus and a response.

medical model The concept of psychological disturbance as a medical problem, where patients are cured by doctors using drugs. See EXISTENTIAL PSYCHIATRY.

medulla (oblongata) The part of the CENTRAL NERVOUS SYSTEM linking the BRAIN and the spinal cord. It helps regulate bodily processes such as blood pressure, heart rate, and breathing.

megalomaniac A person with a MANIA for himself, having a wildly exaggerated view of his own abilities and importance.

melancholia A PATHOLOGICAL extent of a melancholy mood, characterized by sadness and severe DEPRESSION. See INVOLUTIONAL MELANCHOLIA.

membership group In SOCIAL PSYCHOLOGY, the group to which an individual belongs. Compare with REFERENCE GROUP.

memory drum A rotating drum on which a subject is presented with material to be learned.

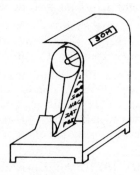

Figure 17 Memory drum. Materials are typed on the tape shown extending behind the drum. The drum presents these materials a line at a time in a controllable order.
(from *Principles of General Psychology*, 4th edition, G A Kimble, N Ganvegy and E Zigler, New York, Ronald Press, 1974, p 415)

memory span The number of items a subject can recall after a single presentation of material. See DIGIT-SPAN test.

memory trace See ENGRAM.

mental age A score on an INTELLIGENCE TEST where items are graded by difficulty and supposedly standardized against chronological age. See INTELLIGENCE QUOTIENT.

mental defective A vague general term used to describe a person who is considered to have insufficient mental development to cope with everyday life and needs special care.

mental set An expectation of, or readiness for, a particular experience.

mere exposure In SOCIAL PSYCHOLOGY, a term introduced by the American scientist Robert Zajonc to explain the phenomenon that, other things being equal, the more familiar people become with objects, words, or pictures they don't know, the more they like them. Mere exposure may thus help to explain the influence of advertising on buying habits.

Merrill-Palmer scale   A test of verbal and manipulative ability for young children.

mesmerism   An early name for HYPNOSIS, named after the 18th century exponent, the Austrian physician Franz Mesmer (who called it animal magnetism).

metapsychology   Used in two senses; either an attempt to include the whole of PSYCHOLOGY in one comprehensive theory, or to go beyond existing theory and observations and speculate about the human condition in general.

middlescence   A term sometimes used in DEVELOPMENTAL PSYCHOLOGY to focus attention on the psychological STRESSES and conflicts of the middle years of life, as well as the unique and positive aspects of this period.

milieu therapy   A form of PSYCHOTHERAPY which focuses on helping an individual by changing his environment rather than his own ATTITUDES or BEHAVIOUR.

Miller Analogies Test   An instrument, using difficult analogy problems, devised to predict future performance in applicants for graduate study.

mind   A vague term used for many centuries in many different ways. As used today by psychologists it most often refers to the totality of organized, mainly cognitive psychological processes.

mind-body problem   One of the most ancient of philosophical debates; what is the relationship of the MIND to the body? Answers to this question have included: 1 they influence each other totally; 2 they don't influence each other at all; 3 mind doesn't really exist; 4 body doesn't really exist; 5 mind and body are really the same thing. And you wondered what philosophers did for a living.

minimax strategy   In GAME THEORY, the strategy of choosing to minimize loss rather than maximizing gain.

Minnesota Multiphasic Personality Inventory   A PAPER-AND-PENCIL TEST containing 550 statements which the subject responds to as being true or false about himself. The pattern of responses is intended to surface certain PERSONALITY characteristics, particularly those associated with a tendency toward psychological disturbance.

mirror writing   writing which looks as if it is reversed but appears as normal when seen in a mirror. Sometimes found in people diagnosed as SCHIZOPHRENIC, but more commonly in children who have a problem with LATERALITY.

misanthropic Hating other people.

miscegenation Technically, breeding between two different genetic stocks. Used as a pejorative term for mixing of the 'RACES', invariably black people and white people, whose differences are much more social than biological.

misogyny Hatred of women.

MMPI See MINNESOTA MULTIPHASIC PERSONALITY INVENTORY.

mnemonics Tricks to aid the memory.

modality In PSYCHOLOGY, a modality usually refers to a particular form of sensory experience, like vision or hearing.

modal personality Literally, the PERSONALITY which represents the MODE of a group. An anthropological term for that hypothetical individual whose personality is typical and illustrative of a particular group or society.

mode In STATISTICS, it is a MEASURE OF CENTRAL TENDENCY; the most frequently occurring value in a group of numbers.

model In SOCIAL PSYCHOLOGY, a person whose behaviour is closely observed. See MODELLING.

modelling In SOCIAL PSYCHOLOGY, a form of learning from observing a MODEL which goes much further than copying or imitating. Children especially may GENERALIZE from the model's behaviour to a wide range of similar behaviours of their own invention.

molar Relating to something as a whole (eg, swimming) rather than to its constituent parts (moving head, arms, and legs in certain ways). Contrast with MOLECULAR.

molecular Relating to the constituent parts of an activity (eg, the head, arm and leg movements in swimming) rather than the activity as a whole. Contrast with MOLAR.

mongolism See DOWN'S SYNDROME.

monogamy A system of marriage, for an indefinite period of time, between one husband and one wife; the NORM in most societies.

monozygotic twins Identical twins who develop from the same fertilized egg or ZYGOTE. Contrast with DIZYGOTIC TWINS.

moral development In DEVELOPMENTAL PSYCHOLOGY there is now a large measure of agreement that the ability to make moral judgments follows a sequence of stages like other aspects of development.

moro reflex   The startle response made by newborn infants, involving clutching movements of the arms and legs.

motion parallax   One of the cues used in DEPTH PERCEPTION; near objects seem to move faster than objects that are further away.

motivation   A general term for any part of the hypothetical psychological process which involves the experiencing of needs and DRIVES and the behaviour that leads to the goal which satisfies them.

motor   PSYCHOLOGY for muscular movement.

Muller-Lyer illusion   A distorted visual PERCEPTION of length.

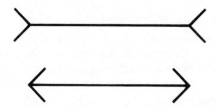

Figure 18 Muller-Lyer illusion where both lines are the same length.

multimodal distribution   A DISTRIBUTION with several MODES.

multiple personality   A rare and dramatic form of NEUROSIS in which REPRESSION leads to the DISSOCIATION of what appear to be two or more complete PERSONALITIES within the same person, as in *Dr Jekyll and Mr Hyde* or *The Three Faces of Eve*. This is what is popularly meant by 'split personality' but is *not* the same as SPLIT-BRAIN (or split mind), and should *never ever* be confused, as it usually is, with SCHIZOPHRENIA.

Murphy's Law   If something can go wrong it will.

N

N Ach   Abbreviation for NEED FOR ACHIEVEMENT.

N Aff   Abbreviation for NEED FOR AFFILIATION.

naive subject   In PSYCHOLOGY generally, a subject who is unfamiliar with an EXPERIMENT; in SOCIAL PSYCHOLOGY, a subject who has been misled as to the real purpose of the experiment. For example, in studies of conformity it would be self-defeating to tell a subject that the point of the experiment was to see how far he would conform to group pressure, so he is given a cover story instead and de-briefed about the real nature of the study when it is over.

narcissism   Excessive self-love in whatever form; characterized by a preoccupation with oneself to the exclusion of others. In PSYCHOANALYSIS, an early stage of psychosexual development where the SELF is the sexual object.

narcolepsy   A disease characterized by an uncontrollable need to sleep.

narcosis   A drug-induced stupor.

nativism   The nature side of the NATURE-NURTURE PROBLEM; in PSYCHOLOGY this doctrine emphasizes the influences of genetic inheritance as opposed to learning, and the INNATE ability to perceive space and time without any prior experience.

naturalistic observation   The scientific observation of events as they occur without trying to manipulate them in the form of an EXPERIMENT or in any other way.

natural selection   DARWINS view of the way EVOLUTION took place, where the fittest or best adapted members of a species in any generation survived in the struggle for existence.

nature-nurture problem   What are the relative influences of HEREDITY and environment on human PSYCHOLOGY?

Necker cube   An AMBIGUOUS FIGURE of a cube.

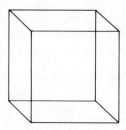

Figure 19   Necker cube

necrophilia   A sexual attraction for dead bodies.

need for achievement   The strongly felt MOTIVATION to achieve, to accomplish ambitions, to be successful. It has been suggested that this motivation is inculcated by careful child-rearing patterns, particularly the fostering of early achievement by mothers in their first born sons. Associated particularly with the American psychologist David McClelland.

need for affiliation   In SOCIAL PSYCHOLOGY, the need to be with other people, particularly when facing the same unpleasant experience. There is some evidence that this need may be related to birth order, with last-born children having least need and first-born children (especially males) having most.

negative reinforcement   Used in CONDITIONING as a way of eliminating a given response by punishing it.

negative transfer   The detrimental effect on later learning of previous learning, because of the different responses required in the two situations. For instance, to steer a boat with a tiller after learning to drive a car. See TRANSFER OF TRAINING.

Neill, A S (1883–1976)   A Scottish educator who founded a school in England called SUMMERHILL with the goal of helping children lead lives free from REPRESSION. Although profoundly FREUDIAN in its orientation, Neill's work has been claimed by HUMANISTIC PSYCHOLOGISTS and educators as an expression of their own principles.

neo-Freudian   A follower of FREUD who also accepts later modifications in PSYCHOANALYTIC theory. Fromm, Horney and Sullivan are the most prominent examples of such modifiers. Early followers of Freud who broke away from this movement, notably ADLER and JUNG, are usually known as schismatics.

neologism   Literally, a new word; sometimes found in SCHIZOPHRENIC speech but more often in scientific and scholarly writing where common words are used in a new way, like CENSORSHIP and PROTOCOL, or where new words are concocted, like BRAINWASHING and TERRITORIALITY.

neonate   A newborn infant.

nervous breakdown   Popular term for a NEUROSIS severe enough to incapacitate an individual and require hospital treatment.

nervous prostration   See NEURASTHENIA.

nesting instinct   The apparently INNATE activity of birds in building themselves a nest. Popularly supposed to apply to people as well. It doesn't.

neuralgia   Disorder of a single nerve that causes sharp, localized, intermittent pain.

neurasthenia A NEUROTIC state of extreme tiredness, weakness and general debility, both mental and physical.

neurology The study of the structure and function of the nervous system.

neuron The cell that constitutes the basic unit of the nervous system.

neurophysiology The physiology of the nervous system.

neurosis A functional psychological disorder with no organic causes whose origins in emotional conflict can often be understood and dealt with by PSYCHOTHERAPY. Neurosis may be manifested as ANXIETY, FUGUE, HYSTERIA, OBSESSION, COMPULSION or PHOBIA.

neurotic Behaviour suggestive of NEUROSIS.

night blindness A weakened capacity for DARK ADAPTATION due to organic disease or vitamin deficiency.

nonconscious ideology The unquestioned assumptions people have about the world which can influence their behaviour profoundly without their being aware of it.

non-directive therapy A therapy which accepts an individual's expression of his needs and conflicts on his own terms, without any preconceived system of interpretation for steering the person in a particular direction. The most notable example of this kind of therapy is CARL ROGERS' CLIENT-CENTRED THERAPY.

nonparametric statistics Statistical methods that may be used when the data does not conform to a NORMAL DISTRIBUTION, ie most data in studies of human behaviour.

nonsense syllables Three-letter combinations that have no meaning for the subject (like ZEJ or TUZ), which are used in studies of memory.

non-verbal communication Direct communication between people by a means other than the spoken word; includes facial expressions, GESTURES, eye contact, hand gestures, and body posture.

norm In STATISTICS, a value representative of a whole group of numbers, such as one of the MEASURES OF CENTRAL TENDENCY (MEAN, MEDIAN and MODE). See also GROUP NORM and SOCIAL NORM.

normal Literally, conforming to the NORM, or standard; as applied to BEHAVIOUR it usually refers to what is expected (the

SOCIAL NORM) or what is generally considered right, proper, or correct under the given circumstances.

normal distribution The DISTRIBUTION of data from a RANDOM SAMPLE of the population. When this data is plotted on a graph it shows up as a symmetrical BELL-SHAPED CURVE with scores clustered around the average and declining towards either extreme.

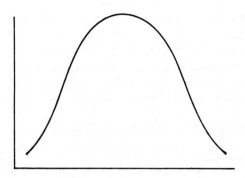

Figure 20 Normal distribution

normative influence In SOCIOLOGY, the process in which other people's anticipated judgment of right and wrong influence someone's behaviour.

nuclear family Mother, father, and 2.4 children.

null hypothesis In EXPERIMENTAL PSYCHOLOGY, the HYPOTHESIS that any difference found between the EXPERIMENTAL GROUP and the CONTROL GROUP occurred by chance and is not significant. The goal of the EXPERIMENT is therefore to reject the null hypothesis and be able to state that the experimental treatment has produced a significant effect.

nymphomaniac A woman with a MANIA for sex. See also SATYRIASIS.

nystagmus An involuntary and often repeated jerking of the eyes to one side followed by a slow return. It occurs normally after the head has been rotated, but can also be a sign of BRAIN DAMAGE.

O

obedience In SOCIAL PSYCHOLOGY obedience often has the particular connotation of conformity to an authority.

object blindness See AGNOSIA.

object cathexis Used in PSYCHOANALYSIS to signify the choice of a love object, usually involving the diversion of LIBIDO from a sexual to a non-sexual object. See also CATHEXIS.

object constancy The way familiar objects are perceived in the same way regardless of changes in the perceptual environment such as lighting, placement, and distance. See also COLOUR CONSTANCY.

objective Usually used to refer to something existing outside of oneself and capable of being experienced with others. Contrasted with SUBJECTIVE.

object libido In PSYCHOANALYSIS, where LIBIDO is directed towards other objects rather than towards oneself as in NARCISSISM.

object loss In PSYCHOANALYSIS, the loss of love from a valued external object.

object permanence According to PIAGET, the understanding acquired by infants during the SENSORIMOTOR STAGE of development that objects continue to exist when they can no longer be perceived. This ability appears to be clearly evident by the age of 18–24 months.

obsession A persistent ANXIETY-provoking idea that one can't seem to get rid of. Compare with COMPULSION.

obsessive-compulsive neurosis A NEUROSIS in which an individual is not only OBSESSED by certain ideas but feels compelled to act on them, often ritually and repetitively, eg, by counting windows or hand washing. In PSYCHOANALYSIS this behaviour is believed to be an effort to relieve GUILT – as in the case of Lady Macbeth's hand washing.

Occam's Razor A principle, suggested by the mediaeval philosopher William of Occam, that has been accepted as fundamental to scientific explanation; if there are rival explanations for a given PHENOMENON the simplest must always be chosen. LLOYD MORGAN'S CANON is fashioned from the same material as Occam's Razor.

occipital   Referring to the back of the BRAIN or skull.

occupational therapy   An adjunct to PSYCHOTHERAPY in hospitals which involves patients in performing useful tasks to help improve their SELF-ESTEEM and feelings of worth.

Oedipus complex   The crux of FREUD's theory of PERSONALITY, the UNCONSCIOUS sexual desire of a son for his mother and consequent jealousy and hatred of his father. Freud considered this COMPLEX to be universal and, if unresolved, to be at the seat of all other NEUROSES, and the cause of a great deal of GUILT. Freud was fascinated by the myth of Oedipus, the tragic hero (of Sophocles, the Greek dramatist) who unwittingly killed his father and married his mother. See also ELECTRA COMPLEX.

oestrogen   The hormone secreted during the period of oestrus when the female animal experiences heightened sexual receptiveness. No such simple relationship between oestrogen and sexuality appears to be true of humans.

old brain   The most primitive part of the human BRAIN which emerged earliest in the course of EVOLUTION. Situated below the CEREBRUM, it deals with reflex actions and basic bodily processes and contains the LIMBIC SYSTEM.

olfaction   The sense of smell.

one-trial learning   Learning that occurs after a single trial or practice.

one-way screen   A window into a room, that looks like a mirror to the subject on the other side. Used by an observer in experimental studies of human and animal behaviour and in the training of PSYCHOTHERAPISTS.

ontogeny   The EVOLUTION and development of an individual organism. Contrast with PHYLOGENY.

operant conditioning   A form of CONDITIONING, introduced by B F SKINNER that attempts to shape BEHAVIOUR by reinforcing or punishing a response which is spontaneously *emitted* (rather than *elicited* as in CLASSICAL CONDITIONING). The emphasis is on an organism operating on its own environment, eg a rat exploring a cage may happen to press a bar. If this behaviour produces the REINFORCEMENT of a food pellet, it will eventually learn how to manipulate its environment to get food whenever it wants. By a careful arrangement of such reinforcements animals can be trained (as any circus will attest) to perform very complex behaviours.

operational definition Defining a concept in terms of the operations or techniques by which it can be studied.

opinion leader A term used in SOCIOLOGY to denote a person of status within a given group whose opinions are highly thought of and who can therefore influence the opinions of other members of the group. See TWO-STEP FLOW OF COMMUNICATION.

optic nerve The nerve that carries information from the eye to the BRAIN.

oral stage According to FREUD this is the first stage in an infant's life when he is mainly concerned with the pleasure he receives from his mouth and its functions. As with all Freud's stages, excessive frustration or satisfaction may leave a person fixated on it, with the eventual result that, in this case, as an adult he may exhibit an oral character typified by a great need for oral stimulation in the form of food, drink, cigarettes, or even talking – especially perhaps when making biting comments.

organizing tendency A term sometimes used in the study of PERCEPTION to describe the way INNATE physiological processes combine with experience to structure our perceptual world.

orgone Wilhelm Reich's concept of a life force, which is most clearly present at the time of sexual orgasm.

orienting reaction Term used in PHYSIOLOGICAL PSYCHOLOGY to describe an animal's BEHAVIOUR in altering its stance to deal with new stimuli in its environment.

outer-directed A term introduced to SOCIOLOGY by the American sociologist David Riesman to describe people who respond to their society mainly by conforming to SOCIAL NORMS, by seeking approval and courting popularity.

overachiever A person who exceeds the level of achievement expected of her. Sometimes used in the field of education to describe someone who tries too hard, ie a person whose ambitions appear to outstrip her abilities. Contrast with UNDERACHIEVER.

overcompensation Producing a greater effort than is needed to overcome a difficulty or resolve a defect. Often used in connection with attempts to overcome an INFERIORITY COMPLEX.

overconforming Sometimes used to describe a person who is excessively slavish to the demands of authority or the conventions of SOCIAL NORMS.

overdetermined In PSYCHOANALYSIS something that has more than one cause; used particularly about the origin of a NEUROSIS or the meaning of a DREAM. As most neuroses and most dreams are considered to be overdetermined the process of analysis usually goes beyond the simpleminded search for a simple explanation to complex PHENOMENA.

overlearning   Learning in which practice or repetition continues beyond the point required for adequate mastery of the task. Overlearning is not usually considered harmful, ie, it is not thought possible to learn something too well.

P

paediatric   Referring to CHILDHOOD health and diseases.

paedophilia   The sexual attraction of an adult to children.

paired associates   A technique used in studies of learning where words are presented to the subject in pairs and afterwards he is given the first word of each pair and asked to recall the second.

paleopsychology   The study of psychological processes supposedly left over from an earlier stage of human EVOLUTION. For example, JUNG's suggestion of a COLLECTIVE UNCONSCIOUS.

palsy   A form of paralysis, often accompanied by trembling.

paper-and-pencil test   Any kind of test or PROJECTIVE TECHNIQUE that requires written answers.

paradigm   A detailed example or MODEL.

paradoxical sleep   A stage of sleep during which there is a great deal of electrical activity in the BRAIN while the muscles are very relaxed and the sleeper is difficult to rouse. The BRAIN WAVES recorded during this phase resemble the pattern found in someone fully awake. There is often a great deal of the RAPID EYE MOVEMENTS associated with dreaming.

parakinesis   A term used in PARAPSYCHOLOGY to describe what appears to be the movement of objects by unknown powers.

parallax   The PERCEPTION of objects as moving when the eyes are moved. Objects closer than the point the eyes are fixed on seem to move in the opposite direction from the eye movements; objects beyond the fixation point seem to move in the same direction as the eye movements. Near objects also appear to move more rapidly than distant objects. Parallax provides important cues in DEPTH PERCEPTION.

parameter Mathematically, a constant in an equation that defines the form of the curve; in PSYCHOLOGY, it is a constant that defines the curve of a psychological function, like learning. The term is sometimes used loosely, and wrongly, as if it was 'perimeter'.

parametric statistics STATISTICS that deal with a NORMAL DISTRIBUTION.

paranoia A PSYCHOSIS characterized by DELUSIONS, especially DELUSIONS OF GRANDEUR and DELUSIONS OF PERSECUTION. Apart from these delusions, which may be vigorously and even plausibly defended, a paranoiac can often behave quite normally.

paranormal Psychological events that do not seem to be explainable by known scientific principles; the subject matter of PARAPSYCHOLOGY.

parapraxis Apparent mistakes of behaviour like FORGETTING familiar names or slips of the tongue; known as FREUDIAN SLIPS in PSYCHOANALYTIC thought.

parapsychology The branch of PSYCHOLOGY that deals with PARANORMAL phenomena as observed by EXTRASENSORY PERCEPTION. The task of parapsychology is to expand the known methods and principles of psychology to include an explanation of paranormal PHENOMENA. From 1927 to 1965 J B Rhine at Duke University directed a parapsychological research laboratory that attempted systematically to study these phenomena. The main criticism of this work is that EXPERIMENTS pointing to the existence of paranormal phenomena could not be replicated outside of Rhine's lab, but see REPLICATION.

Parkinson's Law Work expands to fill the time available.

partial reinforcement See INTERMITTENT REINFORCEMENT.

participant observation A research technique in the SOCIAL SCIENCES where an observer becomes an accepted member of the group he wants to study.

part method A technique of learning in which the material is broken down into smaller parts to be learned separately and then re-combined. Compare with WHOLE METHOD.

passive-aggressive personality A person who expresses anger and hostility by oscillating between extreme DEPENDENCE on, and extreme aggression towards, other people. The term passive-aggressive is also used of behaviour which is passively aggressive. For example, a person arriving late for a meeting with someone he knows will become anxious at his lateness.

paternalism Treating adults like children by withholding from them the power to make decisions affecting their own lives.

pathological ABNORMAL in the sense of diseased or disordered.

patriarchy A society or a social group run by men. Contrast with MATRIARCHY.

patrilineal A society or social group where descent or inheritance is traced through the male line. Contrast with MATRILINEAL.

pattern recognition The process of picking out patterns or shapes from a series of stimuli; used of machines as well as the BRAIN.

Pavlov, Ivan (1849–1936) A Russian physiologist who won the Nobel prize for his work on the digestive system of dogs. In the course of this work he chanced upon a PHENOMENON he could not explain and followed it (reluctantly) out of physiology and into PSYCHOLOGY. What puzzled him was that his dogs began to salivate not only when they were presented with food but even before they were fed, when they recognized the man coming to feed them. The series of EXPERIMENTS he designed in an attempt to find the causes of this behaviour became known as CLASSICAL CONDITIONING, and Pavlov spent the last 30 years of his life working out the applications and the implications of his discovery. Though Pavlov thought he had found a way of studying the BRAIN, rather than behaviour, his work inspired a new American school of PSYCHOLOGY caled BEHAVIOURISM.

peak experience In HUMANISTIC PSYCHOLOGY a rare moment of great emotional power in which a person feels something akin to ecstasy, where he is at one with himself and with the world. A moment of SELF-ACTUALIZATION.

pecking order The hierarchy of status relationships formed among farmyard hens by their process of pecking each other. The most pecked hen has the lowest status. The term is now routinely (and therefore dangerously) applied to status relationships in human groups. Indeed the term 'hen-pecked' has long been part of everyday speech.

pediatric See PAEDIATRIC.

pedophilia See PAEDOPHILIA.

peer group A social group with which one associates on more or less equal terms. Used especially of CHILDHOOD and ADOLESCENCE.

pellagra A nutritional deficiency whose most obvious symptom is a skin disease, but which may also be accompanied by psychological disorders, particularly DEPRESSION.

penis envy   According to FREUD, penis envy is universal in women and leads (in the UNCONSCIOUS of course) to their CASTRATION COMPLEX. Not the most popular of Freud's theories among women.

penology   The study of criminal behaviour and its treatment.

percentile   In STATISTICS, one-hundredth of the total number of scores in a ranked DISTRIBUTION. For example, the 90th percentile is the point below which lie 90% of the scores.

perception   The process by which the BRAIN receives the flow of information about the environment from the sense organs and uses this raw material to help an organism make sense of that environment.

perceptual defence   Defending oneself (one's SELF), or one's EGO from the awareness of unpleasant PERCEPTIONS by misperceiving them as being pleasant or inoffensive, or by not perceiving anything at all.

perseveration   The tendency for an activity to recur, even when there is no apparent stimulus and the activity has no obvious usefulness.

persona   From the Latin word for a theatrical mask; JUNG's term for those CONSCIOUS, surface aspects of PERSONALITY which people employ in their everyday social dealings.

personality   The sum total of all the factors that make an individual human being both individual and human; the thinking, feeling, and behaving that all human beings have in common, and the particular characteristic pattern of these elements that makes every human being unique. Theorists in this field often stress the integrated and dynamic nature of an individual's personality and the important role of UNCONSCIOUS processes that may be hidden from the individual but are at least partly perceptible to other people.

personal space   In SOCIAL PSYCHOLOGY, the idea that the area immediately surrounding a person is felt to be his or her own. The amount of space claimed in this way varies from person to person and from CULTURE to culture, but any invasion of it is taken as a hostile or threatening act. Not to be confused with TERRITORIALITY.

person perception   The process by which people form impressions of others, then flesh them out and make them coherent.

Peter Principle People are promoted to the level of their incompetence.

petit mal See EPILEPSY.

PGR PSYCHOGALVANIC REFLEX. An American equivalent of the British GALVANIC SKIN RESPONSE.

phallic stage According to FREUD, this is the third STAGE in a child's life, between the ages of three and seven, when he is mainly concerned with the pleasure he receives from his sex organs and their functions. As with all of Freud's stages excessive frustration or satisfaction may leave a person fixated on it, so that, in this case, as an adult he may be preoccupied by sexual potency, performance, and conquest. This preoccupation is related to an unresolved OEDIPUS COMPLEX that arises during this stage.

phallic symbol Anything that can be taken as representing the phallus, or penis, such as a pencil. a church steeple, a cigarette or a snake. The term phallus is used in ANTHROPOLOGY and mythology to describe the virtually universal representations of the male organ of generation. The idea of the phallic symbol was taken over into PSYCHOANALYSIS as an aid to DREAM INTERPRETATION, though pop psychologists and the general public have made much more of it than PSYCHOANALYSTS ever did. Like other dramatic psychoanalytic ideas it cannot be used in a simpleminded way, and its origins must be borne in mind. Perhaps that is why JUNG is supposed to have suggested that 'the penis is only a phallic symbol', and FREUD that 'sometimes a cigar is really just a cigar'.

phantasy See FANTASY.

phantom limb The sensation of 'feeling' in a limb that has been amputated. Two complementary reasons for this PHENOMENON have been suggested; the existing SELF-IMAGE or body schema in an adult takes a long time to adjust to a sudden physical change, and the neural links built up between the amputated limb and the BRAIN may still exist in some form.

phenomenology The philosophical viewpoint that advocates the study of direct CONSCIOUS experience, by INTROSPECTION, as it occurs to a particular observer.

phenomenon Anything that appears to an observer; anything that is capable of being perceived.

phenotype The result of the interaction between the GENOTYPE of inherited genetic tendencies and the social environment. There is no way of seeing a person's genotype, for genetic potentialities can only appear in actual BEHAVIOUR. All the behaviour that we can observe, from before birth right throughout life, is therefore a phenotype.

phenylketonuria A condition of serious mental retardation, thought to be hereditary, caused by the failure of the body to metabolize phenylanaline.

philosophy The systematic attempt to understand the ultimate nature of the universe.

phi phenomenon The impression of seeing apparent movement. In its simplest form, two lights flashed on and off in quick succession, with the right time interval between the flashes, will induce people to perceive the light as moving between two points. This ILLUSION is the basis for our PERCEPTION of movement in films, cartoons, and neon light displays. It was discovered at the beginning of the 20th century by the first GESTALT PSYCHOLOGISTS, shortly after the film industry was created.

phobia A morbid NEUROTIC fear of a particular object or situation.

photographic memory See EIDETIC IMAGERY.

phrenology The belief, first proposed in the 18th century, that intellectual abilities could be divined by studying bumps found on the skull. The assumption was that particular areas of the BRAIN dealt with particular abilities, and that the larger the area (and therefore the larger the bump on the skull surrounding it) the greater the ability. Phrenology is now regarded as pseudoscientific, though it did help establish the link between brain and BEHAVIOUR.

phylogeny The EVOLUTION and development of a species. Contrast with ONTOGENY.

physiognomy Formerly referred to the attempt (now considered pseudoscientific) to divine psychological characteristics from the structure of the human face, a practice that sometimes included PHRENOLOGY. Now refers simply to the structure of the face.

physiological psychology The branch of PSYCHOLOGY that deals with the physiological processes underlying BEHAVIOUR.

Piaget, Jean (1896–1980) A Swiss pioneer of DEVELOPMENTAL PSYCHOLOGY, who postulated a series of sequential stages in the developing processes of COGNITION in children; these are the SENSORIMOTOR, PREOPERATIONAL, CONCRETE OPERATIONS, and FORMAL OPERATIONS stages. Piaget was trained as a biologist and retained this orientation throughout his work, believing that the developmental process in children should be allowed to run its own course without encouraging a child to develop at a faster pace. Piaget began his career in psychology by administering INTELLIGENCE TESTS to children. He noticed that when children gave the wrong answers to his test questions they did so in a particular manner; all the children of a certain age gave the same kind of wrong answers to the same questions. By asking children questions about how they perceive things he was able to demonstrate that the world of the child was quite different from that of the adult, both separated from each other by a mutual incomprehension. Though Piaget's research methods and some of his findings have come under critical fire, few psychologists would dispute his great influence in reducing one half of that incomprehension.

pilot study   A small-scale EXPERIMENT or survey set up to see whether a larger one is worth attempting; often used to test the proposed methodology.

PKU   See PHENYLKETONURIA.

placebo   An inactive substance disguised as an active one, eg, a sugar pill, given to a CONTROL GROUP in a drug EXPERIMENT, or to a patient in hospital who would not benefit from an active drug but needs to feel that he is receiving treatment. See also PLACEBO EFFECT.

placebo effect   The reaction to a PLACEBO as though it were an active substance, eg, patients feeling better after being given a sugar pill. The term is sometimes used in a wider sense to refer to a positive response from people when they feel that attention is being paid to them. At this point it sounds very like the HAWTHORNE EFFECT.

plantar reflex   The automatic curling downward of the toes when the sole of the foot is stroked; normally replaces the BABINSKI REFLEX at the age of about two.

plateau   See LEARNING PLATEAU.

play therapy   The use of play in PSYCHOTHERAPY with children, to aid in diagnosis and in treatment; the child is encouraged to experience a CATHARSIS of blocked EMOTIONS.

pleasure centre   An area of the HYPOTHALAMUS which apparently causes sensations of pleasure when electrically stimulated.

pleasure principle   In PSYCHOANALYSIS a key motivating principle of the UNCONSCIOUS which involves the urge to gratify basic

DRIVES immediately and to avoid the experience of pain or 'unpleasure'.

pluralistic ignorance   A social situation in which each individual believes himself to be the only exception to the accepted beliefs or behaviour of his group.

Poggendorf illusion   The visual ILLUSION that a straight line passing behind two parallel lines or rectangles is not actually straight.

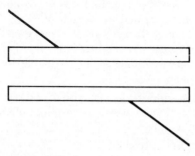

Figure 21   Poggendorf illusion

polymorphism   Passing through different bodily forms in the course of an organism's development, eg, as does a frog or butterfly.

polymorphous perverse   In PSYCHOANALYSIS, the idea that the sexuality of a young child still passing through the ORAL, ANAL and PHALLIC stages of development has no clear outlet, so that his erotic or sexual behaviour would, if exhibited in an adult, be considered a perversion.

population   In STATISTICS, the total number of cases or individuals from which a sample is drawn for study and about which inferences are to be made.

positivism   The philosophical doctrine that scientific knowledge is limited to observed facts and experience.

possession   The feeling of being taken over by some external force. A common sympton of PSYCHOSIS in our CULTURE and religious ecstasy in others.

postconventional morality   The third level of the American psychologist Lawrence Kohlberg's STAGE THEORY of moral development. At this level moral behaviour is governed neither by fear nor convention but by a self-chosen, consciously held system of rational ethical principles. Not everyone achieves this stage of development.

post-hypnotic suggestion   A suggestion made to a person under HYPNOSIS which he carries out after coming out of the trance, supposedly without knowing the origin of the suggestion.

postpartum depression   DEPRESSION following childbirth, perhaps due partly to hormonal changes.

potlatch   A custom of the Kwakiutl Indians of the Pacific North-West who engage in a ritual destruction of their personal property in order to achieve SOCIAL STATUS. The term is occasionally used in SOCIAL SCIENCE writing to refer to ostentatious use of material goods in our own CULTURE.

pragnanz   In GESTALT PSYCHOLOGY, the tendency of any GESTALT towards simplicity, harmony, meaningfulness, and a 'goodness of fit'. For example, a battered old coin seen in a dim light will still be perceived as a circular object.

precognition   A form of EXTRASENSORY PERCEPTION in which a subject appears to have knowledge or COGNITION of a future event which could not be inferred logically.

preconscious   In PSYCHOANALYSIS, something that is not present in CONSCIOUSNESS at a given moment but which can readily be recalled. Compare with SUBCONSCIOUS.

preconventional morality   · According to the American psychologist Lawrence Kohlberg, the first level of moral development, which dominates the moral behaviour of children until after the age of seven. Preconventional morality is characterized by the PLEASURE PRINCIPLE of avoiding pain or punishment and seeking the pleasure of rewards for behaviour that adults judge to be morally good or bad.

predictive validity   See CONSTRUCT VALIDITY.

prejudice   An ATTITUDE, opinion, or belief, with a strong emotional underpinning that makes it largely impervious to reason or evidence to the contrary. The term is usually (though not always) used in a negative sense.

presentation of self   A term associated with the Canadian sociologist Erving Goffman. See IMPRESSION MANAGEMENT.

pretest   See PILOT STUDY.

prevision   A term, very similar to PRECOGNITION, used in the study of EXTRASENSORY PERCEPTION to refer to the experience of 'seeing' future events. Popularly known as 'second sight'.

primacy   The theory that, other things being equal, the first one of a series to be learned is remembered best. Compare with RECENCY.

primal scene   In PSYCHOANALYSIS, the term for one's earliest sexual memory, which is usually taken to be the observation (partial, total or fantasized) of one's parents in the act of intercourse.

primal therapy   A technique of PSYCHOTHERAPY developed in the United States by Arthur Janov in which the therapist first makes the patient feel intensely miserable then encourages him or her to relive miserable feelings experienced in CHILDHOOD but never expressed. When the patient can let go with a 'primal scream' these EMOTIONS are supposedly released, and the way made clear for a healthy adult development.

primary attachments   The earliest and most lasting bonds a human being makes with others.

primary colours   Those colours which are used in combination to produce any other hue: blue, yellow, red, black, and white.

primary group   A small group (such as the NUCLEAR FAMILY) characterized by direct, intimate personal relationships between people who depend on each other for support and for satisfaction of emotional needs.

primary process   In PSYCHOANALYSIS, the UNCONSCIOUS attempts by the ID, governed by the PLEASURE PRINCIPLE, to find ways of obtaining immediate gratification of its needs.

principle of parsimony   See OCCAM'S RAZOR.

prisoners' dilemma   A situation developed out of GAME THEORY and used by SOCIAL PSYCHOLOGISTS in the study of bargaining behaviour. In the game, two suspects are caught by the police and questioned separately about a crime. If one prisoner confesses and the other does not, the squealer is set free and the fall guy takes the rap. If both confess both are convicted, but dealt with leniently. If neither confesses both benefit because they cannot then be convicted.

proactive inhibition   The detrimental effect of previous learning on the recall of later learning. See RETROACTIVE INHIBITION.

probability   In STATISTICS, the likelihood that a given event will occur as compared with the likelihood of alternative events occurring. For example, the probability of obtaining a given number when throwing a six-sided dice is one in six.

programmed learning   A system of self-instruction based on

OPERANT CONDITIONING where tasks to be mastered are broken down into small steps. The subject is given feedback about his mastery of each step as he goes along.

projection In PSYCHOANALYSIS, a DEFENCE MECHANISM where a person UNCONSCIOUSLY attributes to other people feelings he has himself but which are too threatening to the EGO to admit into his CONSCIOUSNESS.

projective techniques Procedures for uncovering a person's UN-CONSCIOUS MOTIVATIONS, ANXIETIES and conflicts. Like the ROR-SCHACH or the TAT they consist of relatively unstructured stimuli which are designed to encourage the PROJECTION of material which would be inadmissable to CONSCIOUSNESS in a direct un-disguised form.

proprioceptors Sensory receptors which deal with information about the movement and orientation of the body. They are found in the SEMICIRCULAR CANALS of the inner ear where they are concerned with balance, and in the muscles and joints where they produce KINAESTHETIC sensations.

protocol The original record of an EXPERIMENT, or the notes and materials of a clinical interview, diagnosis, or treatment.

proximity See CONTIGUITY and CONTINUITY.

proximodistal Literally, 'close-distant'. Usually refers to the process of maturation in humans and animals where the sequence of physical development proceeds from the centre of the body towards the periphery. See CEPHALOCAUDAL.

psyche The Greek term for the life force; translated first as 'soul' then as 'MIND' and now sometimes as 'SELF'.

psychedelic A term usually applied to drugs like HALLUCINO-GENS which appear to sharpen PERCEPTION and expand CON-SCIOUSNESS; also used of colour and lighting arrangements which are supposed to have the same effects.

psychiatrist A physician who specialises in PSYCHIATRY.

psychiatry The branch of medicine concerned with mental ill-ness. The subject matter of psychiatry overlaps to a great extent with that of CLINICAL PSYCHOLOGY, the main difference lying in the training and orientation of the PSYCHIATRIST and the CLINICAL PSYCHOLOGIST. The psychiatrist usually has no training in PSYCH-OLOGY other than in PSYCHOPATHOLOGY and is encouraged to adopt a MEDICAL MODEL for dealing with psychological disturb-ance. The clinical psychologist usually has no training in medicine, cannot prescribe drugs, and tends to regard NORMAL and ABNORMAL behaviour as being on the same continuum.

psychic In general, the properties of the MIND or PSYCHE; popularly used for a person supposedly possessing spiritual or EXTRA-SENSORY powers.

psychical research Popular term for PARAPSYCHOLOGY.

psychic determinism The theory that no psychological event or process is fortuitous or accidental but always has a definite (if UNCONSCIOUS) cause. FREUD proposed this theory as a cardinal, guiding principle of PSYCHOANALYSIS.

psychoanalysis A form of PSYCHOTHERAPY, invented and developed by SIGMUND FREUD. Places a great emphasis on the uncovering and understanding of UNCONSCIOUS MOTIVATION. Any form of psychoanalysis, no matter how far removed it may be from its Freudian origins, would subscribe to this principle. Psychoanalysis is the most arduous and demanding form of psychotherapy, requiring years of (expensive) sessions during which powerful conflicts and EMOTIONS may be raised.

psychoanalyst A PSYCHOTHERAPIST who has been trained in the theory and techniques of PSYCHOANALYSIS. He or she will have been trained initially as a physician, a psychiatric social worker, or a psychologist. A typical training programme may last for four years and will include a personal analysis of the trainee.

psychodiagnostics Originally applied to the interpretation of PERSONALITY through external features like PHYSIOGNOMY and GRAPHOLOGY; now includes perfectly respectable PROJECTIVE TECHNIQUES.

psychodrama A technique developed by the American PSYCHIATRIST J L Moreno. Used in both diagnosis and PSYCHOTHERAPY where a person is asked to act out certain scenes, usually in front of other patients and therapists. These scenes are designed to elicit the patient's personal and social conflicts. See also SOCIOMETRY.

psychodynamics See DYNAMIC PSYCHOLOGY.

psychogalvanic reflex An American equivalent of the British GALVANIC SKIN RESPONSE.

psychogenic Relating to a psychological disorder with no known organic basis.

psychohistory The application of modern psychological thinking to the study of historical events and people. The field has been captured (in both the popular and the academic mind) by the attempted PSYCHOANALYSIS of leading historical figures. This psychobiography began with FREUD's own study of Leonardo Da Vinci and has had a controversial career ever since. However many other lines of psychohistorical enquiry have also been opened up including the history of psychological concepts like MIND, insanity, the UNCONSCIOUS, the history of CHILDHOOD, the SOCIAL PSYCHOLOGY of demographic movements, and the attempt to unravel cause and effect in the change of ATTITUDES over time.

psychokinesis In PARAPSYCHOLOGY, the supposed ability to move objects and affect the physical environment purely by the power of the MIND.

psycholinguistics The study of the relationship between the nature, structure and use of language, and the psychological processes of the users.

psychological field See LIFE SPACE.

psychological warfare The application of psychological thought and research to the manipulation of ATTITUDES in wartime, in an attempt to lower the enemy's morale and increase one's own.

psychologism The view that all studies of human beings (philosophical, political, historical, etc) should be based on PSYCHOLOGY, or even that all questions about human beings are reducible to psychology.

psychologist's fallacy Where a psychologist reads into someone else's MIND what is present in his own.

psychology A subject that is most usually, and briefly, described as 'the study of human and animal behaviour'. No dictionary on the subject would dare leave it there, however, and one such volume (admittedly with claims to being 'comprehensive') goes on and on about it for seven pages. This strategy of surrounding the problem gets the compiler off the hook of having to give an opinion. My own opinion is that it doesn't matter very much – people usually know what you mean by psychology anyway – and pointing out every form of it that you can find doesn't get us much further. 'The study of human and animal behaviour' would be as good a definition as any but for the fact that it focuses attention on the BEHAVIOUR itself rather than the attempt to understand what it's about. But then that's a point that frequently eludes psychologists anyway, so maybe it's not such a bad definition after all.

psychometrics Tests and measures of psychological factors including INTELLIGENCE TESTS.

psychomotor Refers to the effects of mental processes on the actions of the muscles.

psychoneurosis See NEUROSIS.

psychopath See ANTISOCIAL PERSONALITY.

psychopathology Literally, the PATHOLOGY of the PSYCHE the study of psychological disturbances and their origins.

psychopharmacology The study of the effects of drugs on psychological functioning.

psychophysics The study of the relationship between external stimuli from the physical world and the SUBJECTIVE sensations they produce. The psychological processes involved are still as much a part of the subject matter of EXPERIMENTAL PSYCHOLOGY as they were when these problems were studied in the first psychological laboratories established in the 1870s. See WUNDT.

psychosis A psychological disorder which is severe enough to disrupt a person's everyday life and require institutional treatment. Apart from organic causes like BRAIN DAMAGE it has been thought by many psychologists that a psychosis is a severe form of NEUROSIS. More recently there has been a tendency to regard biochemical factors as being a distinguishing characteristic of at least some forms of psychosis.

psychosomatic From the Greek words *psyche* (mind) and *soma* (body); relating to psychological disorders in which emotional STRESS produces physiological symptoms. Illnesses such as asthma and stomach ulcers are widely believed to be psychosomatic, but it has also been argued that, because of the close connection between MIND and body, every illness is psychosomatic at least to some extent.

psychosurgery BRAIN surgery directed at curing a severe psychological disorder.

psychotherapist Someone who practises PSYCHOTHERAPY. He or she is usually a PSYCHIATRIST, a CLINICAL PSYCHOLOGIST, or a psychiatric social worker, but in most places where psychotherapy is practised no special qualifications are legally required.

psychotherapy The use of psychological techniques to treat psychological disturbances. The three main forms of psychotherapy (based on the three main theoretical approaches to PSYCHOLOGY) are BEHAVIOURISTIC, HUMANISTIC, and PSYCHOANALYTIC. There are many variants and permutations of these three approaches.

pubescence The stage of attaining puberty.

Purkinje phenomenon   The PERCEPTION that the red end of the spectrum decreases in visibility in decreasing illumination faster than the blue end of the spectrum. This is why blues seem more vivid than reds at sunset.

Pygmalion effect   See ROSENTHAL EFFECT.

pyromaniac   A person with a MANIA for lighting fires.

Q

Q sort   A technique for rating PERSONALITY TRAITS in which a person is given a large number of statements about himself, or someone else, which he then sorts into piles representing the degrees to which the statements are applicable.

quantal hypothesis   The idea that sensations are not a continuous experience but a succession of separate steps.

quartile   One of the three points on a FREQUENCY DISTRIBUTION which divide it into equal quarters.

queuing   Sometimes used to describe a way of dealing with sensory overload in which all the stimuli but one are put 'on hold' until that one has been processed.

quota sampling   Sampling data from each sub-group of a given POPULATION.

R

r   The symbol for the most common CORRELATION COEFFICIENT.

race   An anthropological term denoting a biological sub-division of human beings with a common genetic ancestry. This common ancestry produces common physical characteristics such as skin colour, facial structure and size. There is no such thing as a pure race; every physical characteristic can be found, however infrequently, in every large human sub-group. It is suggested from time to time that a particular minority sub-group is inferior in INTELLIGENCE to the majority sub-group. At the beginning of this century it was Jews; more recently it has been blacks. There has never been any clear evidence for this viewpoint and a lot of evidence against it. Even if we accepted, for the sake of argument, that there was a pure race and that INTELLIGENCE TESTS measured intelligence, those tests remain educationally, culturally, and socially biased against ethnic minority groups.

racial memory See COLLECTIVE UNCONSCIOUS.

racial unconscious See COLLECTIVE UNCONSCIOUS.

randomize In EXPERIMENTAL PSYCHOLOGY, the random selection of subjects for an EXPERIMENTAL GROUP, or the random presentation of stimuli to the subjects in the EXPERIMENT. This is done so that all individual factors are evened out and will not affect the experimental results.

random-sample A sample chosen at random from a POPULATION (ie, where everyone in a whole population has an equal chance of being chosen) so that inferences can be made to the population from findings about the sample.

rank order A series arranged in order of magnitude either increasing or decreasing.

rapid eye movements See DREAM RESEARCH.

rapport A kind of EMPATHY that a PSYCHOTHERAPIST has for a patient, supplemented by the confidence and trust that the patient has in the therapist. Rapport is essential for successul PSYCHOTHERAPY.

rationalization In PSYCHOANALYSIS, a DEFENCE MECHANISM where a person justifies behaviour about which he has UNCONSCIOUS GUILT feelings.

reaction formation In PSYCHOANALYSIS, a DEFENCE MECHANISM where a person deals with UNCONSCIOUS DRIVES that he finds threatening by reacting consciously in the opposite direction. For example, men with strong homosexual tendencies may behave in a very 'macho' fashion.

reaction time The time elapsed between the presentation of a stimulus and the subject's response to it.

reality principle In PSYCHOANALYSIS, the EGO's modification of the PLEASURE PRINCIPLE that governs the ID. It is the ego's way of striking a balance between what the id wants and what is possible, given the realities of the external environment.

reality testing In PSYCHOANALYSIS, the EGO's practical attempts to follow the REALITY PRINCIPLE.

recency The theory that, other things being equal, the last one of a series to be learned is remembered best. Compare with PRIMACY.

receptor A sensory nerve ending which responds to a particular kind of stimulus; found in the sense organs and the surface of the skin.

recessive gene A GENE that remains latent because it is paired with a DOMINANT GENE.

recidivism Mainly used to describe recurrent criminal behaviour, but also used of repeated psychological disturbance.

reciprocity The principle that a response is produced by a combination of the duration and intensity of a stimulus.

redintegration A principle that is taken to be a prime example of the LAWS OF ASSOCIATION, where the PERCEPTION of a whole unit is accomplished after only a part of it has been presented to the subject.

reference group A sociological term for a group with which a person identifies, and whose GROUP NORMS he follows, whether he is accepted by it or not, and whether he is physically part of it or not. Compare with MEMBERSHIP GROUP.

reflex arc The hypothesized physiological links between a stimulus and a response.

regression A return to an earlier form of behaviour; in PSYCHO-ANALYSIS it is a DEFENCE MECHANISM where a person seeks to deal with ANXIETY and avoid UNCONSCIOUS conflicts by reverting to an earlier stage of development when his problems were solved by more infantile means.

reification Treating an abstract idea as though it had a real, OBJECTIVE existence.

reinforcement Strengthening the likelihood that a given behaviour will recur by rewarding it. This is the basis of all CONDITIONING.

relative deprivation The feeling of being deprived, when a person compares himself with someone else, regardless of the OBJECTIVE reality.

releaser In ETHOLOGY, a stimulus that releases an automatic behavioural response in an organism. See also INNATE RELEASING MECHANISM.

reliability A STATISTICAL term for the internal consistency of a test; the extent to which it can be expected to produce the same result on different occasions.

REM sleep   See DREAM RESEARCH.

repetition compulsion   The COMPULSION to repeat the same behaviour over and over again, the classic example being Lady Macbeth's hand washing.

replication   Repeating an EXPERIMENT over again in exactly the same way (though perhaps in a different place with different subjects); a practice that receives a great deal of lip service in PSYCHOLOGY but which is in fact so rare that special journals have been produced solely for the replication of experimental findings. None of them has survived. There's not much academic mileage in replication.

representative sample   A sample that is intended to be completely representative of the POPULATION from which it is drawn.

repression   In PSYCHOANALYSIS, a DEFENCE MECHANISM and a crucial concept in Freudian theory. The essence of repression is the blotting out from CONSCIOUS awareness of disturbing feelings and impulses arising from the ID. They are submerged in the UNCONSCIOUS – where they invariably get up to mischief. Repression is at the root of many NEUROSES including, most strikingly, AMNESIA. Indeed FREUD considered repression the price we pay for civilization, and psychoanalysis, by making the unconscious conscious, the only way to come to terms with this dilemma. Contrast with INHIBITION.

resistance   In PSYCHOANALYSIS, resistance is the term that describes both the reluctance of material submerged by REPRESSION in the UNCONSCIOUS to surface into CONSCIOUSNESS, and the reluctance of the ANALYSAND, or patient, to allow the ANALYST's probing to uncover areas of unconscious conflict.

response bias   A MENTAL SET to respond in a particular way to certain issues or questions, for example on a questionnaire.

response generalization   Used in studies of CONDITIONING to describe the principle whereby a stimulus producing a particular response can also produce similar responses. Compare with STIMULUS GENERALIZATION.

restricted code   British psychologist Basil Bernstein's term for an inarticulate style of communication consisting of short, often unfinished phrases, limited in ideas and information. Said to be typical of the way working-class parents interact with their children. Contrasted with ELABORATED CODE.

retina   The inner surface of the eyeball which receives visual images and transmits them as neural impulses via the OPTIC NERVE to the BRAIN.

retrieval   The act of remembering something, recalling it from LONG-TERM MEMORY.

retroactive inhibition   The detrimental effect of later learning on the recall of previous learning. See PROACTIVE INHIBITION.

retrospective falsification   Unintentional distortion in remembering previous experiences which is not considered to be caused by UNCONSCIOUS influences.

risky shift   In SOCIAL PSYCHOLOGY, the idea that people will make riskier decisions under the influence of a group than when they are alone.

Rogers, Carl (born 1902)   A leading exponent of HUMANISTIC PSYCHOLOGY and NON-DIRECTIVE THERAPY of which his own CLIENT-CENTRED THERAPY is a leading example.

role   Used in SOCIAL PSYCHOLOGY to refer to the kind of behaviour expected of a given person in a given situation.

role playing   Used in two senses; acting the part of another person in a therapeutic or experimental situation, or playing a ROLE for deliberate effect.

Romeo and Juliet effect   An experimental finding in SOCIAL PSYCHOLOGY that parental opposition leads to the strengthening of a young couple's love.

rooting reflex   The automatic response of an infant to having his cheek stroked; turning his head and opening his mouth.

Rorschach test   The most famous of all PROJECTIVE TECHNIQUES, beloved of cartoonists and comedians. It consists of ten standardized inkblots developed by Hermann Rorschach, a Swiss PSYCHIATRIST. The subject's FREE ASSOCIATION to the inkblots is examined by the tester in the light of certain categories of response which have been standardized over the years. No diagnosis of a person's difficulties would ever be made solely on the basis of a Rorschach test, but many CLINICAL PSYCHOLOGISTS regard it as a useful first step.

Rosenthal effect   A form of EXPERIMENTER BIAS or SELF-FULFILLING PROPHECY in a social setting, suggested by Robert Rosenthal. Rosenthal led a group of teachers to believe that certain children in their classes had high IQs and were expected to do well in the year ahead. The children did do well – though they were all in fact of average IQ.

Rosenzweig test A PROJECTIVE TECHNIQUE in which the subject is shown pictures portraying people in somewhat frustrating circumstances and is then asked what the frustrated person would probably say or do.

rote learning Learning solely through repetition without any attempt to find meaning or order in the materials.

S

Saccadic movement The jumping of the eye from one point of fixation to another, as in reading.

sadism The experience of sexual pleasure through inflicting physical pain. Usually considered a sexual perversion. Named after the Marquis de Sade who did it for a living.

sado-masochism The tendency towards both SADISM and MASOCHISM at the same time. FREUD held that they were, in effect, two sides of the same coin.

satyriasis An OBSESSION with sex in men; the male equivalent of NYMPHOMANIA.

scapegoat The object of DISPLACED aggression. In Biblical times the Israelites sent a pure white goat out to die in the wilderness once a year, on the Day of Atonement, carrying the sins of the people with it. Modern scapegoats are individuals or groups who are blamed for the frustrations of society which are none of their making.

schema A mental model or framework within which new experiences are digested. Extensively used by PIAGET in his descriptions of the way in which children make sense of the world at different stages of development.

schizoid Relating to SCHIZOPHRENIA.

schizophrenia The most common category of PSYCHOSIS and one which covers a wide variety of symptoms and behaviour. The term schizophrenia comes from the Greek words *schizo* (split) and *phrenia* (mind) and this is the source of an almost universal popular misconception. Split mind (or SPLIT PERSONALITY) is the popular term for MULTIPLE PERSONALITY, in which the split occurs between what appear to be different personalities within the same person. The split in schizophrenia however is between the processes of thinking and feeling within the same person, so that the harmony normally found between a person's thought, feelings and actions is disrupted. A schizophrenic may smile, or show no EMOTION at all, when discussing a tragic event, for instance. Difficulties in communication with others, DELUSIONS and HALLUCINATIONS are also common symptoms of schizophrenia.

Schroeder staircase   An AMBIGUOUS FIGURE.

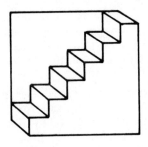

Figure 22   Schroeder staircase

scotoma   A blind area of the RETINA, usually in addition to the normal BLIND SPOT found in every eye.

Seashore test   A series of recorded tests of musical abilities.

second-order conditioning.   See HIGHER-ORDER CONDITIONING.

selective attention   The deliberate focusing of ATTENTION on something to the exclusion of competing stimuli.

self   The self, in HUMANISTIC PSYCHOLOGY, is roughly the equivalent of the EGO in PSYCHOANALYTIC psychology. It refers to that part of the PERSONALITY which is CONSCIOUS of its own IDENTITY over time.

self-actualization   According to the American psychologist ABRAHAM MASLOW, the ongoing striving to fulfil one's capacities that is a sign of psychological health.

self-concept   All the elements that make up a person's view of himself, including SELF IMAGE.

self esteem   How well a person likes herself; how worthy she deems herself to be.

self-fulfilling prophecy   The idea that expectations concerning one's own or other people's behaviour can lead to the expected behaviour appearing, such as in the ROSENTHAL EFFECT. See also EXPERIMENTER BIAS.

self-image   The SELF a person beliefs himself to be. One's self-image is a composite of many things and may bear little relation to any OBJECTIVE assessment of oneself or the assessment of others. The self-image begins very early in life and is probably, to a large extent, physical. This early BODY IMAGE can stay with a person for the rest of his life, so that as a normal-sized (or even tall) adult he may think of himself as small because, when his body image was being formed, he was small in relation to his peers. The judgments of other people are also important in the formation of the self-image, but even though a person's social contacts, and therefore the judgments made of him, may change greatly in later life, he may still think of himself in terms of the earlier judgments.

semantic differential   A technique developed by the American psychologist Charles Osgood for assessing the way in which the same words or ideas are understood by different people. Subjects are asked to rate these terms along dimensions like good-bad or active-passive, and these ratings are then compared.

semicircular canals   Three fluid-filled canals which are located in the inner ear at right angles to each other and pass information about movement and balance to the BRAIN.

sensescence   A term sometimes used in DEVELOPMENTAL PSYCHOLOGY to focus attention on the psychological STRESSES and conflicts of old age and the ageing process, as well as the unique and positive aspects of being old.

sensitivity training   A technique for trying to improve interpersonal communication and the quality of relationships in small groups The orientation of this technique is that of HUMANISTIC PSYCHOLOGY and it is based on the methods and experience of GROUP THERAPY. Group leaders try to facilitate open and honest discussion of feelings within the group. The hope is that any new found sensitivity to one's dealings with other people will carry over to other areas of life.

sensorimotor stage   According to PIAGET, the first stage of cognitive development, from birth to about two years of age. During this stage the infant sees himself (or his SELF) as the centre of the world, but gradually comes to distinguish between SELF and others. The other important achievement of this stage is that of OBJECT PERMANENCE.

sensory deprivation   A situation where people are deprived of the usual stimulation of their senses encountered in daily life. Apparently when people are isolated from sensory stimulation as far as possible in a laboratory they quickly become bored and then start to HALLUCINATE. It may be that when people have nothing in their environment for their BRAINS to work on and make sense of they feel a need to provide their own sensations and make sense out of nothing (Figure 23).

sensory memory The first stage of the memory process, lasting less than a second, during which information is recorded by the sense organs. See SHORT-TERM MEMORY and LONG-TERM MEMORY.

separation anxiety In PSYCHOANALYSIS, an infant's fear of losing his mother. The result of actually losing a mother, or a mother's love, has received widespread attention beyond that of psychoanalysis. See also MATERNAL DEPRIVATION.

serendipity From the island of Serendip in *Gulliver's Travels*; the experience of finding one thing while looking for another; true in varying degrees of major figures in the study of the human condition, like FREUD and PAVLOV. Also found in users of dictionaries.

serial learning Learning material in a particular order or sequence.

servomechanism A system that controls another system. FEEDBACK from the system under control enables the servomechanism to regulate its input so that a constant output is maintained. A thermostat is the usual example given of a servomechanism, but HOMEOSTASIS in the body can also be seen in this way.

sex differences Differences in behaviour or abilities between males and females. As with supposed racial differences, there is no evidence that there are any. What looks like a genetic sex difference in aggressiveness, for instance, is due to a cultural process of learning the SEX ROLE considered appropriate for males or females.

sex-linked trait A genetically transmitted characteristic which is found more frequently in one sex than the other. Perhaps the clearest example is that of red-green COLOUR BLINDNESS which is far more common in men than women.

sex role The BEHAVIOUR a society expects of a male or female on the basis of their sex. As social difference invariably implies PREJUDICE, this is the basis for sexism in society.

shaman An anthropological term for a mystic or medicine man who deals with the supernatural for a living.

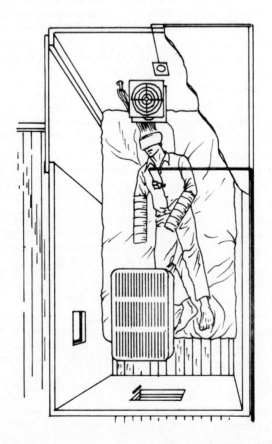

Figure 23 Sensory deprivation. Experimental cubicle constructed to study the effects of perceptual isolation. The subject wears a plastic visor to limit his vision, cotton gloves and cardboard cuffs to restrict what he can touch, and hears only the noise of a fan and an air conditioner above him. Wires attached to his scalp make it possible to record his brain waves. Communication between the subject and the experimenter is possible over a system of microphones and loudspeakers. The room is always lighted and, except for brief intermissions to eat or go to the toilet, the subject lies on the bed twenty four hours a day until he can stand it no longer.

shame culture   A CULTURE which relies on shaming and ridiculing by others to regulate the BEHAVIOUR of a given individual and thus maintain order and social control. Such a culture is vulnerable to people not getting caught when breaking rules, if there is no internalized mechanism of self regulation. Contrasted with a GUILT CULTURE.

shaping of behaviour   A technique used in OPERANT CONDITIONING which rewards any BEHAVIOUR that comes close to what is required, then gradually shapes the behaviour more exactly by reducing the area of rewarded behaviour.

shell shock   The First World War equivalent of what is now known as BATTLE FATIGUE or combat fatigue.

shibboleth   A Hebrew word whose pronunciation was used by one of the ancient tribes of Israel as a password and is used now to denote evidence of one's being 'in the know' or belonging to an 'in' group.

shock treatment   See ELECTROCONVULSIVE THERAPY.

short-term memory   The second stage of the memory process (between SENSORY MEMORY and LONG-TERM MEMORY) lasting for up to 30 seconds. During this period we decide whether to retain the new information in a permanent record (long-term memory) or let it go.

sibling rivalry   Competition between children in a family, usually for the affection of the parents.

signal detection theory   An alternative to the concept of an ABSOLUTE THRESHOLD of sensation which suggests that PERCEPTION (detection) of a stimulus (signal) is related to the sensitivity of the sense receptors and the MOTIVATION of the individual to respond.

significant other   Used by the American sociologist G H Mead to denote a person who is particularly important to us, especially in relation to our SELF-IMAGE. Compare with GENERALIZED OTHER.

Skinner, B F (born 1904)   The most celebrated exponent of BEHAVIOURISM not just in EXPERIMENTAL PSYCHOLOGY, but as a means of running a society. His original technique of OPERANT CONDITIONING was based on the work of PAVLOV and WATSON. He has expounded the social implications of his views in a number of influential works intended for the general public notably *Walden Two* and *Beyond Freedom and Dignity*.

Skinner box   The name given to the apparatus used by B F SKINNER in his studies of OPERANT CONDITIONING. The box must have some mechanism, like a bar or lever, which allows the animal being conditioned to manipulate or operate on its environment.

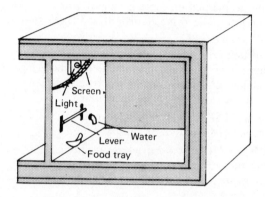

Figure 24 Skinner box
(from *Introduction to Psychology*, 4th edition, E R Hilgard and R C Atkinson, New York, Harcourt, Brace Jovanovich, 1967, p 280)

sleep centre An area of the HYPOTHALAMUS that induces sleep when it is electrically stimulated or removed entirely by surgery.

sleep deprivation When people are prevented from sleeping they eventually experience ill effects such as HALLUCINATIONS and confusions of thought and behaviour. Some scientists engaged in DREAM RESEARCH argue that dreaming is the most important aspect of sleeping and sleep deprivation. Indeed other than dreaming it is difficult to detect any physiological difference between sleeping and just resting.

sleeper effect A term used in several different senses in the SOCIAL PSYCHOLOGY of ATTITUDE change. Its most frequent usage is probably in describing a change in an attitude or opinion after a study has been conducted. This may be one reason for inaccuracy in public opinion polls. The term is also used to describe a more favourable response to a communication after some time has elapsed, rather than the expected decline in the effect of the communication. Sleeper effect is also used to describe the DISSOCIATION between communication and communicator over time so that people may become less receptive to positive sources and more receptive to negative ones.

slip of the tongue See PARAPRAXIS.

social anthropology The study of social systems and CULTURES in different societies, particularly non-literate societies.

social cohesion The attraction within a group for each of its members that helps to bind it together.

social comparison The process of evaluating one's ATTITUDES and behaviour by comparing them with those of other people. In SOCIAL PSYCHOLOGY there is an idea that when people are uncertain of what to do (or think or feel) in a given situation they are more likely to take their cue from other people and conform to their behaviour.

social Darwinism The application to human societies of DARWIN's evolutionary theories of NATURAL SELECTION, where only the fittest members of a species survive. In effect it was (and is) an attempt to justify the existing order by arguing that the rich and successful have evidently been selected by nature to be rich and successful.

social deprivation Where an individual or a group does not have the material benefits common to a given society. The OBJECTIVE aspect of RELATIVE DEPRIVATION.

social distance scale An attempt to measure the degree of social intimacy a person will accept in relation to other groups or individuals.

social-emotional leader The individual who may emerge in a small group as the person who keeps up the morale and facilitates the interpersonal relationships of the group. Compare with TASK LEADER.

social exchange theory See EXCHANGE THEORY OF FRIENDSHIP.

social facilitation The stimulating effect on a person's behaviour of other people – even the mere presence of other people. The HAWTHORNE EFFECT is an example of social facilitation.

social interaction The mutual influence that people have on each other's BEHAVIOUR in a social setting.

socialization The process whereby an individual becomes a social being. Although it is a lifetime process it is particularly important in CHILDHOOD when society is represented by (and through) a child's parents and the rest of his family (Fig. 25).

social norm BEHAVIOUR expected of all the members of a society. The NORM of social behaviour is therefore one definition of social normality.

social psychology The branch of PSYCHOLOGY that deals with

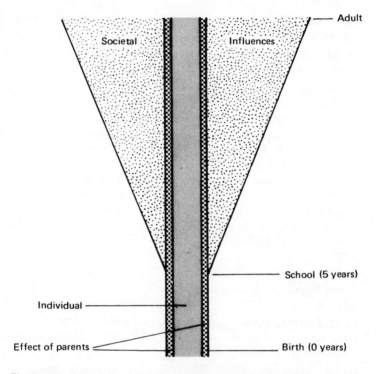

Adult

Societal   Influences

School (5 years)

Individual

Effect of parents   Birth (0 years)

Figure 25 Socialization as illustrated by the Statt Cone

social life, the behaviour of people in groups and the behaviour of individuals in social settings.

social science   Any field of study concerned with people as social beings; to a greater or lesser extent these are generally considered to include ANTHROPOLOGY, economics, history, political science, PSYCHOLOGY, and SOCIOLOGY.

social status   Someone's position in society in relation to, and as determined by, other people.

social stratification   The division of a society into well-defined social classes.

sociobiology   The study of the possible biological bases of social behaviour in humans and animals.

sociocentric   Regarding one's own society as superior to any other and the measure of all things good. It is similar to ETHNO-CENTRISM and usually involves EGOCENTRICITY.

sociology The study of society in general and social organization in particular.

sociometry A term and a technique invented by the American PSYCHIATRIST J L Moreno. It is an attempt to measure what people in a group think and feel about each other.

sociopathic personality See ANTISOCIAL PERSONALITY.

somatising A term sometimes used in PSYCHOTHERAPY to describe the appearance of physical symptoms as a result of psychological STRESS, as in PSYCHOSOMATIC illess.

sour grapes reaction Convincing yourself that something you can't have is not worth having anyway. In CLINICAL PSYCHOLOGY this is called RATIONALIZATION; in SOCIAL PSYCHOLOGY it is seen as an attempt to resolve COGNITIVE DISSONANCE.

spaced practice Any learning with a time interval between practices but which does not necessarily distribute the practices to maximum advantage in the time available, as does DISTRIBUTED PRACTICE.

speaking in tongues. See GLOSSOLALIA.

speech centre An area of the BRAIN particularly associated with the ability to speak. See also BROCA'S AREA.

split-brain technique A surgical technique for severing the connections between the BRAIN hemispheres to relieve, for example, severe epileptic seizures. People who have undergone this operation lose the ability to integrate sensations from both halves of the body and to coordinate the movements of limbs on both sides. There is no communication between the two halves of the brain. But it appears as though each half takes on the functions of the whole brain, resulting in two separate and independent brains, and a double MIND. These effects are entirely the results of a physical operation and have nothing whatever to do with such psychological PHENOMENA as DUAL, MULTIPLE, or SPLIT PERSONALITY or SCHIZOPHRENIA.

split personality See MULTIPLE PERSONALITY.

spontaneous recovery In CONDITIONING, the reappearance of a CONDITIONED RESPONSE which had been extinguished, after a short rest period.

stage theory A theory such as that of PIAGET that conceives of a developmental process taking place in a series of non-arbitrary, sequential, and progressive steps, each of which subsumes all the preceding steps.

standard deviation In STATISTICS, a measure of the dispersion or variability of the scores in a DISTRIBUTION. It is the square root of the mean of the squares of each deviation from the MEAN. Or, to put it simply, the average distance of each score from the mean.

Stanford-Binet The American revision of the BINET SCALE, originally done at Stanford University in 1916 and now the most commonly used individual INTELLIGENCE TEST in the English language.

statistical significance The PROBABILITY that the results of a study could have occurred by chance. The highest probability acceptable to current convention is 5 in 100, or a 0.05 level of significance. See also NULL HYPOTHESIS.

statistics A form of mathematics used on data gathered in studying BEHAVIOUR and by which investigators evaluate their findings and make inferences of wider implication than their study sample.

Statt's Saw There is an exception to every rule, including this one.

stereoscopic vision The PERCEPTION of depth or distance usually due to the merging of the two slightly different images that appear on the RETINA of each eye.

stereotype An oversimplified PERCEPTION of some aspect of the social world. Often tends to be a basis for PREJUDICE.

stimulus generalization Used in studies of CONDITIONING to describe the principle whereby a response produced by a particular stimulus can also be produced by similar stimuli. Compare with RESPONSE GENERALIZATION.

strabismus A squint, produced by lack of coordination of the eye muscles which does not permit both eyes to focus on the same point.

stranger anxiety A fear of strangers (or, more particularly, of unfamiliar faces) that appears in infants at about eight months of age.

stratified sample A frequently used technique for mass polling. It involves the division of a POPULATION into sub-groups and taking a RANDOM SAMPLE of each sub-group.

stream of consciousness A term introduced by the 19th century American psychologist William James, whose brother Henry James is considered to be the first writer of 'stream of consciousness' novels. The term was intended to emphasize the continuous nature of a person's CONSCIOUS experience as opposed to a contemporary trend in PSYCHOLOGY to divide CONSCIOUSNESS into separate units for study.

stress   Physical and psychological strain, usually lasting for a period of time, which threatens the ability of a person (or an animal) to go on coping with a given situation.

stroboscopic effect   A visual ILLUSION of movement produced by a rapid succession of stationary images, as in films. (See PHI PHENOMENON.) The term is more specifically used of the effect obtained when a moving object is illuminated by a rapidly flashing light.

Strong Vocational Interest Blank   A questionnaire about a person's interests which is matched with the reported interests of people in different vocations.

structuralism   A school of PSYCHOLOGY, closely associated with WILHELM WUNDT, which emphasizes the contents of the MIND as it appears to INTROSPECTION and the mental framework or structure that contains these contents. Contrasted with FUNCTIONALISM.

subconscious   Something that is not quite CONSCIOUS but can readily be made conscious. The term is most often used in a physiological sense, to denote an area of the continuum running from full conscious AWARENESS to deep sleep. Its PSYCHOANALYTIC equivalent is the PRECONSCIOUS, but *not* the UNCONSCIOUS with which it is popularly confused.

subculture   Usually denotes a CULTURE within a culture, which shares the main features of the parent culture while retaining special characteristics of its own.

subjective   Usually used to refer to something existing inside oneself and not capable of being experienced by others. Contrasted with OBJECTIVE.

sublimation   In PSYCHOANALYSIS, a DEFENCE MECHANISM in which unacceptable UNCONSCIOUS impulses are channelled into consciously acceptable forms. For FREUD this was society's main way of handling REPRESSION. It is certainly the most socially acceptable of the defence mechanisms.

subliminal   Referring to stimuli below the LIMEN or THRESHOLD of CONSCIOUS PERCEPTION.

Summerhill   The school dedicated to freedom from REPRESSION founded by A S NEILL.

superego   Literally the 'over I' in Latin; according to FREUD one of the three main aspects of the PERSONALITY. Like the ID, with which it is always in conflict, the superego is basically UNCON-SCIOUS. It is the INTERNALIZATION of restrictions on the impulses of the id, as reflected in the values and standards of BEHAVIOUR required by society in general and parents in particular. It is the equivalent of a conscience in a system of ethics.

superordinate goal   In SOCIAL PSYCHOLOGY, a goal which is beyond the capacity of any one group by itself and requires the active cooperation of more than one group. It is regarded as a means of promoting good relations between groups.

surrogate   Someone who takes the place of another psychologically. For example, an older sister as a mother surrogate, or a PSYCHOTHERAPIST as a father surrogate. In PSYCHOANALYSIS, the term is often used of someone or something, usually represented UNCONSCIOUSLY in a DREAM, whose function is to conceal the true IDENTITY of the person or object causing powerful feelings.

survey research   A technique of gathering data from large numbers of people by the use of questionnaires and sampling methods.

survival value   Referring to a physical or behavioural characteristic which increases the probability of survival of an individual or a species.

symbiosis   A biological term referring to the permanent DEPENDENCE of two organisms on each other for their mutual survival. Sometimes used more loosely by psychologists to describe two people whose relationship appears to foster their individual NEUROSES.

symbolic interaction   A sociological way of approaching SOCIAL PSYCHOLOGY. It emphasizes the part played by language, gestures and other symbols of social interaction in our conscious attempts to form ourselves and our world, and it regards our human qualities as the products of that social interaction.

sympathy   The ability to feel with someone. An emotional experience as opposed to EMPATHY.

synapse   The junction at which a nerve impulse passes from one NEURON to another.

Szondi test   A PROJECTIVE TECHNIQUE consisting of 48 photographs of psychiatric patients which the subject is asked to divide into two groups, those he finds attractive and those he finds unattractive. His choices are supposed to be a clue about his needs and conflicts regarding other people. This used to be quite a popular technique but is now rarely used.

T

taboo An anthropological term for BEHAVIOUR that is forbidden by a CULTURE. Usually has magical or religious associations, but often used in a wider context for any important social prohibition. In PSYCHOANALYSIS it often refers to the REPRESSION of socially unacceptable sexual impulses, like INCEST.

tabula rasa Latin for 'blank slate'. An idea going back at least as far as Aristotle, in the fourth century BC, that the MIND at birth is blank and all later contents are put there by experience.

task leader The individual who may emerge in a small group as the person who tries to keep the ATTENTION of the group focused on its task and who tries to see that the job gets done. Compare with SOCIAL-EMOTIONAL LEADER.

TAT See THEMATIC APPERCEPTION TEST.

teaching machine An instrument for aiding PROGRAMMED LEARNING.

telegraphic speech The form of speech used by children of 18 months to two years of age where only the key words in a phrase are used (with the 'ifs', 'ands' and 'buts' missed out).

telekinesis See PSYCHOKINESIS.

teleology As used in PSYCHOLOGY, the study of psychological PHENOMENA with the assumption that they have some goal or purpose, and the search for that goal or purpose.

telepathy Communication between two MINDS, or knowledge by one person of another's thought, without the aid of the known senses. A form of EXTRASENSORY PERCEPTION.

tender-minded A description by the American psychologist William James of one side of a PERSONALITY dimension (the other being TOUGH-MINDED). It implies an idealistic, optimistic, and religious kind of outlook.

territoriality The concept, developed mainly in ETHOLOGY, that certain animals will stake out territory, which they will defend, for their own use or the use of their group. The suggestion is that this tendency is INNATE in these animals. BEHAVIOUR that appears to be similar in humans should be labelled with great caution. There is no evidence that such behaviour is innate in human beings. See also CROWDING BEHAVIOUR.

testosterone   A male sex hormone secreted by the testes.

T-group   A form of SENSITIVITY TRAINING.

thanatology   From THANATOS, FREUD's term for the death force; the study of the way people deal with death and dying.

thanatos   The Greek word for death which FREUD adopted for his concept of the death force or death INSTINCT; a tendency towards self-destruction. Contrasted with EROS.

Thematic Apperception Test   A PROJECTIVE TECHNIQUE developed by the American psychologist Henry Murray containing ambiguous and vague drawings (usually of one or two human figures) about each of which the subject has to make up a story. The themes that may emerge from these stories are then used to diagnose areas of emotional conflict or concern in the subject.

therapeutic community   A therapeutic situation in which the total environment is seen as aiding a patient to overcome psychological disturbance, on the basis that it was the patient's former total environment which led to his disturbance in the first place.

therapy   See PSYCHOTHERAPY.

third force   A term used for those psychologists who subscribe neither to a PSYCHOANALYTIC nor a BEHAVIOURIST view of the human condition but to a broadly HUMANISTIC one.

Thorndike-Lorge count   A list of the relative FREQUENCIES of some 30,000 English words. Its development kept a lot of graduate students gainfully employed in the 1930s.

thought-disorder   A disturbance of a person's usual thought processes; often taken as one symptom of PSYCHOSIS.

threshold   See ABSOLUTE THRESHOLD and JUST NOTICEABLE DIFFERENCE.

tip-of-the-tongue phenomenon   The failure to recall something that we know very well, which is on the 'tip of the tongue'. This is due to a failure of retrieval from LONG-TERM MEMORY storage rather than the REPRESSION of painful memories.

T maze   The simplest form of MAZE, in the shape of a letter 'T'.

token economy   A procedure of BEHAVIOUR THERAPY employed in a mental institution where tokens are used as rewards to reinforce desired behaviour. The token are exchanged later for something the patient wants.

tolerance for ambiguity   The ability to live with a situation that is not clear cut, where different interpretations of what is happening are possible and where the outcome is unclear; the ability to accept complexity in human affairs without seeking simplistic solutions. High tolerance for ambiguity is usually seen as a sign of psychological health and maturity.

topological psychology A form of FIELD THEORY, focusing on the interaction between an individual and his LIFE SPACE. Proposed by KURT LEWIN.

totem An anthropological term for a living thing, or a symbolic representation of it, which is worshipped by a group of people as a protecting spirit.

tough-minded A description by the American psychologist William James of one side of a PERSONALITY dimension (the other being TENDER-MINDED). It implies a materialistic, pessimistic, and irreligious kind of outlook.

tracking Making the necessary adjustments to follow a moving object; often used of the eye movements of an infant or a patient with suspected BRAIN DAMAGE.

tradition-directed A term introduced to SOCIOLOGY by the American sociologist David Riesman to describe people who respond to their society mainly by following the rules and customs laid down in its traditions.

training analysis The PSYCHOANALYSIS undergone by someone training to be a PSYCHOANALYST.

trait Any enduring characteristic of a person.

transactional analysis A form of GROUP THERAPY in which the interrelationships of the group members are analyzed in terms of their transactions with each other as 'parent', 'child' or 'adult'.

transcendental meditation An ALTERED STATE OF CONSCIOUSNESS achieved by relaxation and meditation on a MANTRA.

transference In PSYCHOANALYSIS, the process whereby the patient transfers his feelings about other people who are very important to him on to the ANALYST. It is regarded as a normal, if not essential, part of the analytic process. The analyst, by refusing to play the ROLE assigned him, can show the patient what he is doing and help him uncover the importance of the original person.

transfer of training Where the learning achieved in one situation is transferred to another situation. This can be positive (knowing Spanish aids the learning of Italian) or sometimes negative (knowing how to steer a car is detrimental to steering a boat with a tiller). See LEARNING SET.

transsexuality   Someone's feelings that he or she is really a member of the opposite sex in the wrong body. Transsexuals are the people who request sex change operations. Not to be confused with TRANSVESTISM.

transvestism   The COMPULSION to dress in the clothes of the opposite sex, or the experience of sexual excitement when dressed as a member of the opposite sex. The 'bearded lady' of the old circus freak shows was a transvestite. Not to be confused with TRANSSEXUALITY.

trauma   A physical or psychological shock resulting from an injury or violent incident.

trial and error learning   The step-by-step learning over many trials characteristic of most animal learning and much human learning, and the basis for CONDITIONING procedures. A very laborious process compared to INSIGHT LEARNING.

truth drug   A narcotic (like sodium amytal) that has the effect of causing drowsiness and reducing INHIBITION (and possible REPRESSION) so that the subject may reveal information which he would not do if fully CONSCIOUS.

t-test   In STATISTICS, a test for deciding whether the MEANS of two groups of scores are significantly different.

two-step flow of communication   The idea that the mass media of communication first influence the OPINION LEADERS in a community who in turn influence the opinions and ATTITUDES of others.

U

unconditional positive regard   In CARL ROGERS CLIENT-CENTRED THERAPY, this is the ATTITUDE of total acceptance that the therapist has to show the CLIENT for the therapy to be successful.

unconditioned reflex   See UNCONDITIONED RESPONSE.

unconditioned response   An INNATE reflex or a response that has not been learned previously; so called when produced by a given stimulus at the beginning of the CONDITIONING procedure. For example, the unconditioned response of salivation in response to food may be used to induce salivation in response to a bell.

unconditioned stimulus   A stimulus that produces an UNCONDITIONED RESPONSE at the beginning of the CONDITIONING procedure. For example, food producing salivation.

unconscious   The most important concept of DYNAMIC PSYCHOLOGY and in particular of PSYCHOANALYSIS; the region of the PSYCHE that contains impulses and desires which are too threatening to be allowed into CONSCIOUSNESS and from which they have been REPRESSED or INHIBITED from entering. The effects of this repression and inhibition are expressed in consciousness as NEUROTIC BEHAVIOUR. While FREUD did not discover the unconscious (and never claimed to have done so) he systematically probed the dynamic mechanisms involved in its relationship with the conscious psyche, and did more than anyone to expose the great amount of irrationality in human affairs.

unconscious motivation   Any MOTIVATION of whose origin, or even existence, a person is unaware.

underachiever   A person who fails to meet the level of achievement expected of her. Sometimes used in the field of education to describe someone who doesn't try hard enough, ie, a person whose abilities could take her beyond her ambitions. Contrast with OVER-ACHIEVER.

undoing   In PSYCHOANALYSIS, a DEFENCE MECHANISM where a person engages in some (usually ritual) activity which he hopes will magically undo an earlier act of his that is disturbing him. This is seen as the mechanism behind OBSESSIVE-COMPULSIVE NEUROSIS, the classic example of which is Lady Macbeth's guilty hand washing.

utilitarianism   The PHILOSOPHY that the practical usefulness of something is the sole criterion of its value, a philosophy that has greatly hindered the advance of understanding in the study of human BEHAVIOUR.

V

validity   See CONSTRUCT VALIDITY.

variable   A condition or factor, usually in an EXPERIMENT, that is capable of changing or being changed.

variance In STATISTICS, the square of the STANDARD DEVIATION; used to measure the spread of scores in a particular test or EXPERIMENT.

venereal disease Disease transmitted through sexual intercourse. In some instances, if left untreated, BRAIN DAMAGE can result.

verbal learning Learning the uses of words.

vicarious trial and error A BEHAVIOURIST term to describe the substitution of mental trial and error for physical trial and error in animals who stop at a decision point in a MAZE. It is an attempt to get round the difficulty that the animals appear to be thinking, a strict TABOO to a strict behaviourist.

Vigotsky test A test of the ability to form concepts which involves sorting a series of blocks by colour, shape, and size; named after a leading Russian psychologist, pioneer in studying the relationship of thought and speech to intellectual development.

visual cliff An apparatus used to study the existence of DEPTH PERCEPTION in human and animal infants. The purpose of the apparatus is to produce the optical ILLUSION that part of the floor falls away sharply, to see whether the infant will have the depth perception necessary to be convinced by the illusion and refuse to venture off the 'cliff'.

voyeurism Literally 'looker' in French; someone who gains most sexual pleasure from watching sexual activities or activities associated with sex, like undressing.

VTE See VICARIOUS TRIAL AND ERROR.

W

WAIS See WECHSLER ADULT INTELLIGENCE SCALE.

Watson, J B (1878–1958) The founder of BEHAVIOURISM, who later left academic life for a lucrative career in advertising.

Weber's Law As formulated by the 19th century Germany physiologist, this was one of the first products of PSYCHOPHYSICS. The law concerns the relativity of one's judgment of stimulus sensations, stating that the JUST NOTICEABLE DIFFERENCE between two stimuli is a constant proportion of the original stimulus. This law holds good only for the middle range of stimulus intensities.

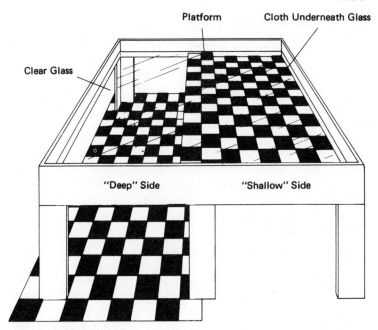

Figure 26 Visual cliff

Wechsler Adult Intelligence Scale One of the most widely used INTELLIGENCE TESTS for adults, combining performance and verbal ability testing.

Wechsler-Bellevue Scale See WECHSLER ADULT INTELLIGENCE SCALE.

Wechsler Intelligence Scale for Children A modification, for use with adolescents and older children, of the WECHSLER ADULT INTELLIGENCE SCALE. The STANFORD-BINET is the test most widely used with younger children.

Weltanschauung A German term usually translated as WORLD VIEW.

Weltschmerz A German term literally meaning 'world sorrow' and which denotes a sentimental kind of worldly weariness.

Wernicke's area The area of the BRAIN first identified as a SPEECH CENTRE.

whole method A technique for learning in which the material is learned as a whole on each practice or repetition. Compare with PART METHOD.

WISC See WECHSLER INTELLIGENCE SCALE FOR CHILDREN.

wish fulfilment   In PSYCHOANALYSIS, an attempt to fulfil an impulse or desire, usually by FANTASY and in DREAMS.

withdrawal   Removing oneself from a situation of conflict or ANXIETY and seeking refuge elsewhere such as in alcohol, drugs, sex, or even work.

wolf boy   See FERAL CHILD.

word association test   A technique for probing areas of psychological difficulty which a person may have REPRESSED. The subject is asked to give immediate responses to a list of pre-selected words, while his answers and the time taken to react to each stimulus word are noted.

word count   The relative FREQUENCY of appearance of different words in a given amount of spoken or written language. See THORNDIKE-LORGE COUNT.

working through   A process of PSYCHOTHERAPY, and in particular PSYCHOANALYSIS, in which the patient goes over and over his basic problems with the therapist until he gains some insight into their origins and dynamics and achieves the ability to cope with similar situations by himself.

world view   A way of understanding the world; a PHILOSOPHY of life.

Wundt, Wilhelm (1832–1920)   The first self-proclaimed psychologist, as opposed to physiologist or philosopher, who in the 1870s founded the first experimental laboratory. The programme of research now called PSYCHOPHYSICS and followed by experimental psychologists was intended to support his STRUCTURALIST theories. But it is often said that twentieth century PSYCHOLOGY became dominated by BEHAVIOURISM and PSYCHOANALYSIS as a reaction against Wundt's thinking.

X

x and y chromosomes   The CHROMOSOMES which determine sex. In most species, including homo sapiens, females have two x chromosomes and males one x and one y.

xenophobia   A PHOBIA about strangers.

Y

Yerkes-Dodson law An idea concerning the relationship between MOTIVATION and learning which states that strong motivation will interfere with learning that is complex but facilitate learning that is simple.

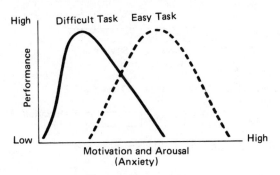

Figure 27 Yerkes–Dodson law

Young-Helmholtz theory The best known theory of colour vision which suggests that the RETINA contains three types of colour receptors, for red, green, and blue, and that all other colours perceived are reducible to some combination of these three.

Z

Zeigarnik effect A finding by a GESTALT PSYCHOLOGIST named Bluma Zeigarnik that subjects are more likely to remember details of experimental tasks during which they were interrupted than those they were allowed to complete. The effect has been claimed for many non-experimental situations where someone is interrupted.

zeitgeist A German term literally meaning 'spirit of the times.' It is used to denote the prevailing social and political mood of an era, the conventional wisdom, the fads and fashions in every-

131

thing from hair length to PSYCHOLOGY. A zeitgeist affects the emotional and mental life of everyone who lives through it, and is thought to have similar effects on people of a similar age group, thus providing one basis for a GENERATION GAP.

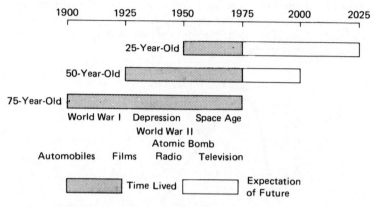

Figure 28 Zeitgeist and changes over time

zero-sum theory In GAME THEORY, a situation where one person's losses are another's gains because there is a finite amount to be won. (The gains and losses in the game add up to zero.) This situation has been suggested as a MODEL for the distribution of rewards in our society.

Zollner illusion A visual ILLUSION in which parallel lines appear to diverge.

Figure 29 Zollner illusion

zoomorphism The interpretation of human behaviour in terms appropriate to animal behaviour.

zoophobia A PHOBIA about animals.

zygote In humans and higher animals, the cell formed by the union of the sperm cell and the egg cell of the parents and from which a new individual will emerge.